A FIELD GUIDE TO
THE YETTIE

A FIELD GUIDE TO
THE YETTIE

AMERICA'S YOUNG, ENTREPRENEURIAL TECHNOCRATS

SAM SIFTON

talk
miramax
books

HYPERION

NEW YORK

ISBN: 0-7868-8609-9

FIRST EDITION

10 9 8 7 6 5 4 3 2 1

To Tina Brown and Robert Wallace at *Talk* magazine, where the article that occasioned this book first appeared. To Danielle Mattoon, Tom Ackerman, Davia Smith, Armin Harris, Tobin Levy, James Lochart, Mike Cooke, and Mike Wolf, also at *Talk*, who worked on that piece with me and did much in the months that followed to help it grow. To Jonathan Burnham, Kristin Powers, and Hilary Bass at Talk Miramax Books, for wise editing and invaluable help throughout the process. To Marvin Putnam at Barnes, Morris, Klein & Yorn, for beneficial counsel in all senses of the word. To an extremely able reporter, Knox Robinson, for yeoman's work in Silicons Alley and Valley alike. To countless e-mail correspondents and don't-use-my-name interview subjects from here to Sand Hill Road and back. To Kristine Larson for her photography and Helene Silverman for her design. To Brent Cox at the Dog & Pony Show in New York City, where some of this material first found its calling. To Manny Howard, Tom Griffith, and Mary Ryan. And most of all to my wife, Tina Fallon. She's the one true thing.

Brooklyn, New York
September 2000

Sam Sifton is a senior editor and writer at *Talk* magazine.

CONTENTS

1

INTRODUCTION:
MEET THE YETTIES

THE FIRST GOOD look I had at the yettie was in a bar on the eastern edge of Silicon Alley in downtown Manhattan. The realization that I was looking at an entirely new cultural phenomenon, one as mannered and unique as its evolutionary forebears in the world of business culture, came to me slowly, like fog lifting off the San Francisco Bay. But then—*contacting host…loading…document complete*—there he was! There were a legion of him, and dozens of her. All of them crowding into this bar in Manhattan to coalesce in front of me as this new, new thing: a fellow standing there in full Banana Republican mufti, with his head shaved close, yapping on a silver Nokia cell phone and tapping his skateboard-shoed foot against the gray slate floor. It was about 10 at night. The average age of the bar's patrons was in the neighborhood of 28. "Stock!" the young man exclaimed into the phone. "I'm so psyched!"

There were two possibilities about this young man—and one certainty.

One possibility was that he was employed at an Internet company. Next to him, the young man had a black computer bag stitched with the name of a company headquartered in Silicon Valley, down in the dusty hinterlands of San Francisco, in San Jose. It was roughly used, as if it had been traveling. The young man had a *second* bag, too, of the sort bike messengers wear, for the rest of his gear. There were a couple of magazines sticking out of this second bag, and they were business magazines, devoted to what's come to be called the New Economy. The magazines were The *Industry Standard* and *Fast Company*. The "Marketplace" section of the *Wall Street Journal* was in this bag as well, along with a Frisbee and a tangle of thin computer cables. These items marked the young man as a technocrat almost as surely as a helmet and a turncoat would have marked a fireman.

The second possibility about this young man was that he considered himself, in some deeply self-aware manner, hip. His shoes were laced loosely, just so. His glasses were dramatically small and angular and black. His watch was symmetrically understated and large; it was a timepiece of the stealth-wealth variety. You couldn't immediately say that it was an expensive watch, but you had the feeling it might be, which was entirely the point. His shirt, though rumpled, bore the name of an expensive clothing designer on its lower hem. He wore it the way your uncle Chester might model his chamois hunting shirt after a long day selling bulk candy at Kmart. He wore it *real* casually. And you could see, when he bent down to return his mobile phone to his bag, and the fabric of the shirt went tight against his back, that the T-shirt he was wearing beneath it bore the logo of an Internet company, a dot-com.

The certainty about this fellow rang down from the ceiling of the bar then, like a clarion call: This young man was a *yettie*.

"Yettie" is an acronym. Yetties are *young*. They are *entrepreneurial*. They are in their behavior and spirit *technocrats*. Those involved in the New Economy are fond of acronyms. The culture of the New Economy is rife with acronymic handiwork. Old people—which is to say anyone much over 30, or anyone who was introduced to computers only in or after his collegiate years—know a few of these. They may know WWW, for "World Wide Web." They may also know URL, for "uniform resource locator": in other words, a Web "address." They may understand DVD, for "Digital Video Disc," the shiny pancakes that have started to appear, and multiply, at their local Blockbuster, and which will eventually replace that tired old rental technology, the video cassette. And, they almost certainly know IPO, for "initial public offering." Or, as some bears put it in the days following the New Economy's first black day, in April 2000, "imminent public obscenity."

There are many, many more acronyms. The New Economy is an ARE; it is an acronym-rich environment. (For help in negotiating it, I have included a chapter about the ARE at the end of the *Field Guide*.) There is even an acronym for all the acronyms. "It's all about the TLA," a person involved in the computer industry told me once. We were talking about Internet culture. I said, "The TLA?" He laughed. "Three-letter acronym," he replied. This guy was a young, entrepreneurial technocrat, too. He was a yettie.

The yettie represents a new branch on the business culture's evolutionary tree. It is a limb that is growing at an astounding rate. A blue-sky report put out in late 1999 by the University of Texas with funding from Cisco Systems estimated that between the first quarter of 1998 and the first quarter of 1999, the number of Internet-related American jobs had rocketed from 1.8 million to 2.5 million, generating some $523.9 billion in revenues for the year, up from $322.5 billion in 1998. In contrast, the national paleo-economy, even buoyed as it had been by an exuberant bull market, grew just 6 percent during the same period. The tech-heavy Nasdaq market index, even after suffering a severe beating on April 14, 2000, still finished the year ending April 17 up 42.5 percent; the Dow Jones Industrial Average, by contrast, rose only .8 percent in the same period.

Still, the April, 2000 Nasdaq crash sent a foul stench through the yettie community. It seemed to represent the end of the first great boom of the New Economy, one that had allowed seemingly anyone with a company name ending in .com to reach insane heights of market capitalization. It seemed to some to represent the end of days. But as a tree bends to the wind and grows higher despite all, the New Economy managed to rally as the warm sun of summer promised at least the possibility of continued market swell. Indeed, a new economic principle, the "preservation of uncertainty," began to take hold in the minds of investors, as if to rationalize all doubts. As better information and technology reduce uncertainty about the future, explained John Browning and Spencer Reiss in their June roundup of the *Wired Index*, a market index of 40 publicly-traded stocks, "investors bid up prices—but rising prices inflate valuations, restoring uncertainty. When superefficient markets respond to this push-pull, they do so immediately and mercilessly." Volatility? No problem! Volatility is the very point itself. This is the New Economy. The yettie resides at its heart.

REMEMBER THE *yuppie?* The yuppie, that gel-haired '80s go-go boy, seems so picturesque and distant now. Like the yetties I saw that night at the bar, yuppies were "young." They were "urban" (or "upwardly mobile," depending on the demographer with whom you talked). They were also "professional," which meant they worked in professional-school careers. They went to business school, to law school, to medical school—sometimes to law school *and* business school. They achieved this schooling, and then they went to work on Wall Street, where their diplomas hung on the walls of mahogany-trimmed offices.

They were clearly identifiable as a type. Yuppies wore, at work, the raiments of the professional class. They had yellow power ties and suspenders. They had brightly shined cap-toe oxfords. They had fancy pens in the vest pockets of suits that looked almost bespoke, as if the designs, carefully drawn in a 250-year-old shop on Jermyn Street in London, had been sent through a fax machine to Honduras and assembled by the thousands.

Yuppie women wore business rig modeled on the masculine example: Paul Stuarts, tragically paired with running shoes over tennis socks over hose, and ruffled blouses rising to Bo-Peep cravats tied tight at the neck. They played weekend golf and bought gold scarab brooches on business trips abroad and just generally got ahead in the world on the notion that they *could,* if they worked hard enough. After all, they'd gone to Wharton.

But then the stock market crashed, in October 1987, and just like that the yuppie was gone, consigned to the thrift store of stereotype along with preppies and hippies and all the others who had come before. Bankers, by about the mid '90's, might as well have called themselves bank tellers, for all the respect accorded them by the world without. Typical response of a yettie, when confronted by a banker friend at the start of the new century: *What are you doing working at a* bank, *dude?*

The death of the yuppie left a vacuum in the annals of American business-cultural stereotype. Generation X attempted to fill it, with its dire predictions about slackers and heroin and bands. "This is the first generation in America that will *never* have more money than its parents," went the popular very-late-'80s refrain. "The job market is *tight,* maaaaan." Generation X took to the couch and smoked pot. "Here we are now," sang Kurt Cobain on Nirvana's *Nevermind,* released in the fall of 1991, "entertain us." Well. These people are creeping up on 35 now, and woe is them if they aren't pulling heavy stock options at Sawthelight.com. Because Generation

X disappeared, too. A recovered economy, a suicidal lead singer, and the sudden belief in an inalienable right to at least a 20 percent return on investment helped kill it dead.

That, and the growth of the Internet and the New Economy. And with that growth, the birth of the yettie.

Who the Yettie Is

Very roughly, a yettie is an employee of an Internet company who cannot explain to his mother exactly what it is he does for a living. (Or to *her* mother, for that matter. In most cases throughout this book the pronouns—if not the costumes and attitudes—are interchangeable. I'll let you know when they're not.) The company the yettie works for may be on its way to an IPO. It may be putting itself in a position to be purchased by a much larger company—Microsoft, for instance—for a lot of money, or for a lot of stock, or for a lot of money *and* stock. The yettie's employer might in fact *be* Microsoft—or Sun, or Oracle, or Dell, or any of the established giants of the New Economy. The yettie might be a product development tech for Amazon, in the lawn and patio division. Or a campaign execution specialist for Internet marketing platforms at Oracle. He might be a CEO. Or a temp. He mountain-bikes on his rare days off.

In college, the yettie may have majored in dance. He may have majored in economics. Or computer science. Physics. Or literature. Certainly the yettie is smart. Often wickedly smart. He has played and worked on computers since the third or fourth grade, for which he endured playground taunts. In middle school, he may have used his computer, a primitive modem, and Mom's phone line to screw around with the big computers at the local community college (ALL CLASSES CANCELED! reads every screen in the school one morning. I HAVE A BONER!!), or to receive free phone service from

AT&T. He may have spent time playing violent video games in real time over the Internet, with friends and strangers alike. In college, he may have bought TAG Heuer watches in bulk from one e-store, only to sell them at a profit at another, before heading off to a dorm party.

The yettie's political opinions are likely to be libertarian in nature, conservatively retrofitted to allow for what he sees as his inevitable massing of wealth. Privacy is of the utmost importance to his philosophy.

It is of the utmost importance to his bottom line as well. In Silicon Nation, which comprises not just California's Silicon Valley and New York's Silicon Alley but cities from Seattle to Boston to Los Angeles to Austin and back, nondisclosure agreements between individuals and companies that are nascent, huge, or anywhere in between litter the streets like leaves in autumn. (Nondisclosure agreements, in the ARE, are called NDAs.) Keeping mum about ideas is for many yetties entirely the point of their existence, insofar as a great number of the biggest Internet companies have been founded on what seem in retrospect to be flatly obvious developments. Indeed, in 1995, it was the simple desire for relatively "private" e-mail, needed so that they might communicate secretly about starting a business while at work, that led two Apple employees, Sabeer Bhatia and Jack Smith, to invent Hotmail, a free e-mail service that can be accessed over the Web. Hindsight speaks clearly about the import of this idea: *Of course that will sell.* On New Year's Eve in 1997, Bhatia sold Hotmail to Microsoft for stock worth $400 million; by May, 2000, the company had more than 66 million active users and was signing up new accounts at a rate of around 270,000 a day. To the yettie, privacy can be extremely lucrative.

The yettie is between the ages of 24 and 50, but is probably closer to the former. Yetties are media-savvy: Tickers on their monitors at work and their laptop screens or mobile phones bring them the latest news and market updates. Their apartments are strikingly underfurnished, though if they're successful yetties, with long money in the market and good cash in the bank, the apartments are larger than one might expect. They will remain underfurnished, at least for the first few years of wealth: A successful yettie has no time to buy taste and isn't, besides, at home that much anyway.

A drug-consuming yettie smokes marijuana, delivered to him by a dealer he contacts via pager. (Drug dealers are the only Americans left with pagers.) Cocaine is in the provenance of public relations executives and nightclubbing celebutainment types. Yetties use it all the same. Yetties drink a lot of coffee, barista-brewed. The yettie has a mobile phone, maybe two, on which he can read his e-mail. He has an instant-messenger service imbedded into his computer, for communication with friends. He rarely uses a "land line" telephone.

The yettie is in possession of stock options. Also of stock. He may or may not be a vested member of his company, but the yettie is almost certainly more wealthy on paper than he is in fact. There is a phrase that comes from the Wall Street of yore that some yetties repeat to themselves like a mantra, in order to appear both wise and modest: *Stock is one thing. Real money only arrives when you sell.* In the days that followed the Nasdaq index's catastrophic correction, these words took on a bitter realism for many in the yettie world. But it did nothing to quench the true yettie's molten desire. Better days would come again.

Greed is neither good nor bad to a yettie. It is a simple entitlement, one that comes to the smart, the hardworking, the wise, the lucky, the prescient—to the yettie.

Yettie Archetypes

Within the yettie world, there are close to 20 distinct yettie types. These range from the mammoth-brained geek CEOs who built the New Economy out of strings of numbers and rods of hope to the nerdy young ectomorphs who keep it standing through winds of change. A yettie can be a programmer, or a cheerful public relations executive; he can also be a business development guy, or a content-providing workhorse with a small one-bedroom apartment out in the sticks. He can be a lawyer, or a refugee from the world of brick-and-mortar retail sales, or a journalist, or a marketing rep.

There are, however, three archetype yettie strains, from which the rest of the yettie world descends. These are the Nerd Made Good, the Neo-Yuppie Prepster, and the Mouse Jockey. I'll address those last two in a moment. But as the schoolyard bullies used to put it: first, the nerd. Upon the nerd— smart and bespectacled, standing alone on the playground in fourth grade, taunted by classmates—was the dot-com geek built. And upon that geek was raised the yettie in all his puzzling forms.

The Nerd Made Good

Those who programmed computers at Microsoft in the 1980s were manifestly unhip. They drank Jolt cola to stay awake for days at a stretch and ate frozen pizza to survive. They washed infrequently. They cared about things that much of the rest of the world considered weird: computers, for instance, and science. These "nerds" are now in their 40s; some are millionaires many times over. They and their descendants—young men from India and Dubuque and the New Jersey shore, who role-played in fantasy games as children and hacked code for fun in college, or young women from professorial families in Boston and Terre Haute and Portland, who read Dragonlance novels as children and became the model for Daria on MTV: These are the wealthy or soon-to-be-wealthy new engines of Internet expansion.

Gone are their pocket protectors, their "Goth" phase, the ignominy they faced in 11th-grade gym class. The Nerd Made Good now has a PalmPilot and new snowboarding boots (and maybe an aerobatic biplane or Ferrari Testa Rossa too). He works as a software programmer or translation specialist or product manager or server farmer or CEO. The Nerd Made Good has spent a great deal of time alone, in front of glowing screens. It has paid off for him handsomely.

The Neo-Yuppie Prepster

The second sort of building-block yettie type is one we can identify as the Neo-Yuppie Prepster yettie. This yettie often labors in a position that defies simple job description: something along the lines of "vice-president for e-presence." The category is filled with square-jawed ex–lacrosse players who might have ended up partners at Skadden, Arps in Manhattan, or Pillsbury, Madison in San Francisco had it not been for the siren song of dot-com. These yetties are managerial, in the main. They often end up running the company—or bolting from the company to start their own, most often in partnership with some Nerds Made Good. They make more money doing that than they ever would have as a member of the bar or running a fund at Daddy's firm, and they get to thumb their noses at "antiquated" business models in the process. Because even if he is a lawyer or a venture capitalist (that's VC, in the ARE), this sort of yettie believes himself a new kind of lawyer or venture capitalist.

Though one no less ready for wealth than his predecessor. Indeed, more so. The sense of the new entitlement runs through this yettie's blood like oxygen. He makes business deals over games of ultimate Frisbee. He considers that fact "awesome."

The Mouse Jockey

The final yettie building block is the Mouse Jockey. These are what used to be called, back in the dark ages of the mid-1990s, alternakids. Mouse Jockeys design Web sites, provide content for Internet publications, write code, and can while away full days playing Quake with their officemates. Their precursors during the yuppie era were in bands and defined themselves as—or, more properly, were defined as—"grunge." For the Mouse Jockeys, though, the Internet *is* rock 'n' roll. Their laptops are their guitars.

In the world of the Mouse Jockey, we find the last gasp of neo-primitive tattoos and piercings, chop-socky clothing choices, and hacker rage. Also, as fortunes rise, mid-century Modern furniture. And a down-loaded-from-the-Web soundtrack that runs heavily to electronica and hip-hop. We see in the Mouse Jockeys rampant creativity, and occasionally a fiercely reactive Luddite strain that manifests itself in appreciation of books and vinyl recordings. And satire, self-hate, raw animosity, confusion: It was classic Mouse Jockey behavior that led, in the early months of 2000, to the development of a San Francisco poster campaign devoted to a Web site called BlowTheDotOutYourAss.com, featuring advertisements for such "companies" as "FreeRectal ExamsOnline.com." (Perhaps predictably, given the state of the New Economy at the time, there was immediate investor interest in the Blowthedotoutyourass "company.")

Mouse Jockeys are women almost as often as they are men. They own two bicycles: one for the city, the other for mountains. Mouse Jockeys bemoan their relative poverty compared to their peers. They eat out—or order in at work—four or five nights a week. At 30, they may lose the Radiohead T-shirt and trade up to Prada. Or they may not. Geek is good.

The Yettie World

The world of the yetties is a complicated ecosystem. That is to say, it is a tangle of yettie types and interrelationships existing both in what's called the meatspace of real life and in the geekosphere of work. Of course, all of the yettie types are dependent on the others for survival. Their relationships are entirely symbiotic, in both the real-life and business senses of the term. For the yettie, naturally, the two are indistinguishable.

Some simple examples. Without a fellow to do the marketing of his site, the CEO of Hogcalling.com has no way of "branding" his business effectively, so that when the public thinks "bacon" it thinks, singularly and to great profit, "Hogcalling.com." And without the CEO, the marketing fellow has nothing to market but himself. He may know the Web as well as he does the neighborhood in which he was raised, but he cannot *master* it without the CEO's idea: online bacon! (For that matter, he cannot master the Web—nor can the CEO master it—without the Programmer's code, or the PR Bunny's public relations work, or the Mouse Jockey's slavish devotion to the task of maintaining the site, or on and on.) Likewise, without the venture capitalist, our CEO is just a guy with an idea to sell bacon over the Internet. But without the yettie CEO, the VC is investing in—what? Brick-and-mortar frozen-yogurt franchises? E-commerce is what the VC wants now. Could you sell the bacon to another *business?* he might ask, justly worried about the future of niche-driven consumer e-tailing. But he'll proffer the money. Brick-and-mortar business plans are seen as very 19th century just now. Everyone on the Internet needs everyone else. The very word implies it.

These symbiotic relationships among yetties exist across both the smallest and widest divides in yettie culture. As an example, a Mouse Jockey with a shared house in Austin, Texas, who spends his days testing code for www.dell.com is flatly dependent on Dell Computing for his paycheck and the experience the company offers him. But though Dell could fire him at any moment and hire a new geek just off the bus from Cal Tech, it won't—because, well, just check out that Mouse Jockey's Dell Computing tattoo on his shoulder, not to mention the unasked-for prospectus for a new line of Dell workstations that's on his screen at 12:45 A.M. on a Thursday. The Mouse Jockey works to make Dell money, and to make it for himself, because he strongly believes in the mission of Dell: "To be the most successful computer company in the world." (That is, by the way, Dell's actual mission statement.) The Mouse Jockey *believes,* and all yettie CEOs need yettie believers to make their companies flourish, as much as they do the VC and the marketing and the codewriting and all the rest.

The world of the yettie is—as an anthropologist might say—a closed system. The yetties speak their own language (languages plural, if you count programming languages and slang vocabularies, and you should). They observe their own idiosyncratic beliefs. On some level they assert a unique and important understanding of life itself. Yetties share a culture.

In the Wild

I was in an airport in the late winter of 1999, as a cluster of yetties virtually stormed the gate of a flight bound for San Francisco, just above Silicon Valley. There was a guy near me in the terminal looking at them with the same expression you might get watching a pride of lions fell a giraffe. There was total, enraptured horror on his face. The guy was in his 50s, with razor-cut white hair and an executive's golf-tanned complexion. His suit was perfectly tailored, and his briefcase was made of the finest leather. He turned to a stranger.

"Who *are* these people?" he asked.

The Field Guide to the Yetties is a small attempt to answer that question—an endeavor charged with the desire to paint a picture of yettie culture for those who live outside it. The parents of yetties, for instance, or a yettie's older sisters, who went to work doing corporate litigation at Cahill, Gordon in New York, instead of starting E-thongs.com and making a bundle in the Internet underwear game like the kid of the family, who's worth $15 million and change. Also friends of yetties, perplexed at their childhood chum's recent wealth and charity and receipt of fawning notice in the local newspapers and burgeoning New Economy magazines—since, after all, that guy failed English in high school and spent most of college pounding away at gibberish on a monitor stained nicotine-yellow with Drum smoke. What's he doing driving a Porsche Boxster now?

Indeed, the job of *The Field Guide to the Yetties* is to explain yetties to *anyone* who wonders about these informally dressed youngsters who walk and talk with an air of self-entitlement that's at times shocking even to the most rabid '80s corporate raider. Even to yetties themselves, waiting on the next round of financing, the stroke of luck, the smile of Fortune.

There will be in what follows bits of history and occasional attempts to divine the future. There will be, obviously, a great deal of categorization. Stereotyping is perhaps the better word; this book is the product of months of fieldwork amid

American yetties, and the particulars of each yettie subtype are built out of the shared tastes, interests, styles, and worldviews of dozens of individuals.

The yetties are brought to us on streams of data and waves of venture capital, then swaddled in casual hipster wear. They are the new smart set! The future of business and culture alike! With *A Field Guide to the Yettie* you may Pygmalionize yourself into one and share in their vast and apparently ever-growing fortunes. Or you may choose to venture forth and identify a yettie in the wild, in order to cast approbation—or violent deprecation—where it is due. Or you may indeed simply choose to observe the yetties in their natural environment—as you might a flock of particularly interesting, potentially endangered, birds.

2

FROM THE TOP DOWN:
YETTIE CEOS

MICHAEL J. SAYLOR, who is the president and chief executive officer of an Internet company called MicroStrategy, is in many ways the model of a yettie CEO. He is both a Nerd Made Good and a Neo-Yuppie Prepster. Saylor was graduated from the Massachusetts Institute of Technology. He used to be very into *Star Trek* and keeps figurines of little dragons and gnomes and such in a case in his living room—which, he has explained, are gifts from his mother. He is a nerd, but with the lightest hint of jocko about him. While at MIT, Saylor was in a fraternity and served as an undergraduate ROTC officer. (Saylor's father was in the Air Force, and Saylor was raised on military bases around the world.) Saylor has the face of the frat-boy officer class, but it is covered by a nerd's complexion: It is pasty, almost soft beneath its angles.

Saylor is 35 years old, and in the summer of 2000, he was worth something close to $1.5 billion.

Saylor used to be worth much more than this amount. But because of some changes the Securities and Exchange Commission required of MicroStrategy's accounting practices, and because of a particularly lousy response from Wall Street to the result of those changes, Saylor watched his company's stock fall 140 points in a single day in late March, which took from him personally $6 billion in net worth. He had only recently announced his intention to pledge $100 million to begin a free Internet university.

A reporter for *The New Yorker*, Larissa MacFarquhar, wrote a very good story about Saylor in the wake of this terrible day. MacFarquhar had spent a goodly amount of time with Saylor in the months leading up to his $6 billion hemorrhage. The loss was a blow to Saylor, she reported, but not a killing one. ("If we take an eighteen-month perspective," he told her on March 22, the day after his stock's crash, "it's just a lot of publicity, right?") In MacFarquhar's story, Saylor expanded on his business beliefs. MicroStrategy sells data-mining software that companies use for "decision support," and Saylor believes that this software will change the world—or, more properly, *should* change the world, if it's sold as he wants it to be, to individuals as well as corporations. Saylor also spoke with MacFarquhar about his "responsibility" as CEO of MicroStrategy and explained why he appears to have such a difficult time relaxing, or even enjoying himself outside of the confines of work. (For much of the three years after he moved his company to Virginia from Delaware, where he founded it at age 24, Saylor lived in a house absolutely devoid of furniture.)

"If I go to a movie theater on a Saturday night by myself," Saylor told MacFarquhar, "while I'm sitting there I'll be thinking, 'You have a $15 billion responsibility, you have time to watch a movie?' What if that three hours is the margin of success? If I were to calculate the true value of my time to the company, there's no way I could justify doing anything other than working."

No way to justify it! Saylor's intense fervor seems to lie near the very core of what it means to be a yettie CEO. Entrepreneurial zeal! You have *got* to believe. Absolute and total self-absorption in the pursuit of success—and of world-changing success at that—is a real marker of those who sit at the very top of the yettie heap.

Although leisure's important, too. Not long ago, a friend of mine received an e-mail from a friend of his, a guy who started an Internet company a few years ago—and who last year sold that company to a larger concern for something in excess of $30 million. He's CEO of a new outfit now, also an Internet company. There are plans afoot for an eventual IPO—even in the wake of the Nasdaq's shaky spring. Of course there are. This friend of my friend's had sent my friend the e-mail to invite him up to see some property he'd just purchased and to go hunting and fishing with a bunch of other friends. The CEO would be flying a guide in from somewhere to help out and instruct those who'd never cast a fly or fired a shotgun. This guy is 29 years old. He just bought a new Lexus SUV. He is having a yacht built.

The yettie CEO may be a Saylor-like figure, a messianic leader of men and companies, extraordinarily devoted to his cause. He may be, more simply, a guy who had a great idea in a market that didn't require of it profits, only the promise of them, and who saw in these facts a way to become very rich— a methodology that is fast running out of steam. He may be an opportunist. He may also be a sleazebag. Or a perpetual adolescent. Or a figurehead. But if he is at the top of an Internet company, he will almost certainly fall into one of three distinct yettie-CEO types.

The Cyberlord

THE MOST dominant strain of yettie CEO is what the Internet social critic Roberto Verzola has called with some venom the Cyberlord. Cyberlords, like all yettie CEOs, are members of what could be called the Internet culture's propertied class. They control either information or, as Verzola has put it, "the material infrastructure for creating, distributing, or using information." Verzola assumes the posture of a vintage Marxist then, and gets kind of angry: "Cyberlords are rent-seeking members of the capitalist class," he seethes.

You bet they are, Roberto! That's how they got to be rich. You want to type a letter to someone on your laptop, then print it out, or e-mail it? Pay Microsoft, pay Apple, pay Dell, pay Hewlett-Packard, pay AOL, pay! You want to find out how well your widget is selling in malls in the Southwest as opposed to the franchise stores in Boston or New York? You want to find out if there's romaine lettuce fresh at the Schnuck's on the corner? Pay Michael Saylor and he'll hook you right up. That's what MicroStrategy does, after all, and the intellectual property rights for how to do that belong to him, and to his company. Pay rent and he'll let you use his devilish little system all night long.

The Cyberlords, unlike most yetties, spend a good deal of time dressed in suit and tie. (Most yetties only wear suit and tie on the inside, over their souls.) They wear them for meet-ings with members of the Old Economy—which still has plen-ty of money despite its apparent decrepitude—whose approval they crave despite the changing sands of American wealth. (This desire for tacit endorsement goes both ways, it's worth pointing out. When AOL announced its planned merger with Time Warner in January 1999, it was no real coincidence that AOL chairman Steve Case wore a jacket and tie, while Time Warner honcho Gerald Levin opted for an open-necked sports shirt of the sort more often worn by professors of zoology. The message was clear from both sides: *I'm like you. Like me!*)

Cyberlords are white men, in the main, but they do not have to be. That last is important. *They do not have to be*. They only have to dress as if they are. As the novelist and Silicon Valley journalist Po Bronson has pointed out, his voice echo-ing across the canyons of the media, which is the New

1. **Big, geeky, clear glasses.** The Cyberlord looks in the mirror and thinks: Like Gates himself!

2. Although entirely inadvertent, the slight **curve in the collar** marks the Cyberlord as ever so slightly absent-minded—and ubernerdy!

3. **Business suit 101.** Bought off the rack a year before the 1998 IPO, which made him, on paper, the single richest man ever to have attended River South High School in Adversity, N.Y. Subsequent market fluctuations have done nothing to alter this status.

4. **World phone**, with earphone mike. He's calling in for the children, on his way from his G4 to the bathroom at the San Francisco Airport.

5. **Simple analog watch.** A gift from his father, who ran a dry-goods business in Adversity, and who died the evening of the IPO of an apparent heart attack.

6. **Wedding ring.** Married Cindy from marketing five years ago, before he was rich. He does not cheat.

7. **Stainless-steel attache.** Within it is a hi-lightered copy of Gates's *Business @ the Speed of Thought*, two other business self-help books, and notes for a speech given at the Wharton School of Business: "…This is a revolution, friends. We're carrying rifles, we are shooting from the trees… Recontextualize the global impact of modular service business transactions!" Also a **Mont Blanc pen** with which he signs contracts, and a **tiny Dell laptop** with which to compose and send the nearly 200 e-mails he prosecutes each day, mostly between 11 P.M. and 2:30 A.M.

8. **Cap-toe oxfords.** Cindy buys the shoes, or has them purchased for him, he's not sure. They have a lot of staff these days. In any event, they're shiny, and the Cyberlord likes this fine. GOOD SHOES = SHAREHOLDER CONFIDENCE is one of the Cyberlord's favorite secret aphorisms.

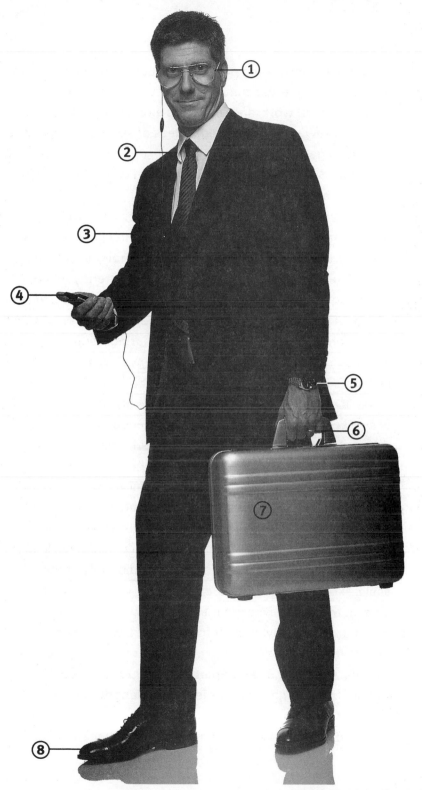

Economy's chief trading partner, the success-oriented environment bred by Internet culture has led to a fundamental shift in the nature of work, and of culture along with it: The New Economy rewards success regardless of skin color, regardless of class, regardless of gender. You can arrive in America from India with $123 in your pocket and return with a billion. The economy allows it: Brains will out.

The Cyberlord almost certainly has a background in technology and an intimate understanding of the product he is hawking: *He built the product.* He is also probably a great student of new business practices and of insta-trendy management books and seminars that allow him, he believes, the possibility of great power over his employees, business partners, and potential clients. When he's not wearing a suit, his pants continue to display pleats, long after they have fallen from fashion.

He is also an entrepreneur. All yetties are entrepreneurs, of course, but to the Cyberlord, entrepreneurship is more a divine calling than a mere facet of his personality. The Cyberlord assumes massive risk in the hope of enormous profit. The adjectives are important. They are why he went to business school. And why he dropped out.

The Cyberlord is probably single. (He may be married to an employee; as the joke has it, he doesn't need to pick up women—he hires them.) He is possessed of only limited social skills. He communicates primarily via e-mail and can be cruel in these missives. He may, in the wake of an IPO or a sale, purchase a toy or a gift for himself: a Gulfstream airplane, for instance, or a large collection of working model helicopters, or a ship, or a complete set of *Superman* comics. He will not talk about these acquisitions at length. He may later build a dream house, which will invariably combine elements of Scandinavian design with hints of both Dungeons &

Dragons and *The Jetsons*. He will continue to drive the Nissan Sentra he got from his sister when she finished medical school until someone tells him not to do so any longer because it looks weird, him driving that car. Nerd!

He may sleep at work, under his desk. He does not keep an extra shirt in his desk drawer. His desk drawer is pinioned shut anyway, by a drift of white papers and memos and old copies of *Wired*. He has one best friend, whom he has known since college, where for the first time in his life he was actually celebrated for his intelligence and for his ability to write programs for computers. This person works for him now, as either his chief operating officer or his chief technology officer. Sometimes, if the friendship was struck in business school, as his chief financial officer.

Employees fear the Cyberlord and revere him as serfs did the beneficent Lord of the Manor.

The Game-Over Guy

THE SECOND sort of yettie CEO is the quintessence of Nerd Made Good, and though he occupies a smaller category than the Cyberlord, he is a wildly important member of the yettie culture: He is a tie to its dark, geeky, fantastical past. The Game-Over Guy is a game designer. The company he founded—and runs as CEO—manufactures and sells those games for personal computers, often via the Web.

The Game-Over Guy is from Texas, where many game manufacturers have their headquarters. He lives just outside Austin, in the same ranch house he lived in five years ago, before he was rich. He is very, very good at the games Doom and Quake, which he considers, despite his efforts to supplant them with his own company's, to be the very best "first-person shooter" games that have ever existed. John Romero,

(1) **Kool guy shades** that vibe to the Game-Over Guy as somewhere between Oakley insouciance and granny-glass chic.

(2) **The hair, man!** No scissors have touched these strands since 10th grade. Wash it once a week and pull back for meetings.

(3) Mom's religious, which is cool even if she sounds like one of the *Peanuts* parents most of the time; the Game-Over Guy thinks it's necessary for people to have **philosophies**. His is Dungeons & Dragons filtered through Doom refracted through his own game designs. He wears the cross because it looks cool and Mom likes him for it.

(4) "You know what this is a **key** to, dude? My Lamborghini Diablo V12, which goes 0-60 in 3.9 seconds and cost me $300,000. I drive it to work every day it's not in the shop. Every day!"

(5) **Gold Rolex**, like Fred Durst's! Games *sell*, dude. They sell a *lot*.

(6) **Black jeans**, always. In the left front pocket, between the Game-Over Guy's greasy fingers, is a token from a strip club out on the fringe of the Las Vegas Strip, where the company's last management retreat occurred. Beneath that a roll of new $50 bills, for office betting. Also a ten-sided die from high school—he was the Dungeon Master.

(7) Custom-tooled **cowboy boots** made by the third cousin of an apprentice of Charlie Dunn, in Austin, Texas. The stitching on them bears the name of his game and its rallying cry: LET GOD SORT 'EM OUT! The boots are really, really uncomfortable.

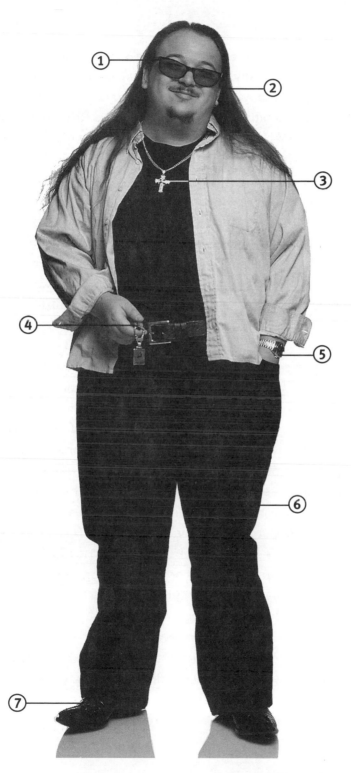

the rock star-ish co-creator of those games, is a real hero to the Game-Over Guy. In private, he will slag Romero viciously, as a ninth-grader who longs to make varsity will slag the popular, erratic senior who plays quarterback. He wants the position. He wants it very badly. He keeps toys in his office, little fetishes to inspire him to greatness and to remind him of the past: plastic monsters, ray guns, pools of rubber blood.

The Game-Over Guy can work or play on a computer for a 16-hour stretch with no visible strain to his eyes or body. He can do this two or three times in a week without harm to his life schedule. He will in fact enjoy himself, as he does on the occasional visit to a local strip-mall strip club with his younger employees. If someone sends the Game-Over Guy a challenging e-mail, declaring that the sender can beat the Game-Over Guy at the Game-Over Guy's own game, in real time, over the Internet, the Game-Over Guy will accept the challenge. If he loses, he will almost certainly hire the challenger. Recruitment, he feels, is one of his strong suits as a CEO.

The Game-Over Guy drives the fastest and most rocket-like car he can secure; he'd like a Ferrari like the one Romero has, but has a Lamborghini "for now." He listens to heavy metal. He wears sunglasses with purple lenses. His hair is long, greasy, tied back for work, let down for the strip club or the occasional shower. The Game-Over Guy is very single. He likes systems, order, rules. He likes to break them down. He read Tolkien. He read *Watership Down* and *Lord Foul's Bane*. *The Matrix* was bullshit to him, unreal, though he loved it all the same. He is something of a self-denying intellectual.

The Game-Over Guy enjoys the attention of those who love his game, and therefore *him*. He also enjoys the attention of the market, which can reward him handsomely for his efforts. These attentions, lavished on those who have created their personae out of the anger and creativity of youth, lead to both the Game-Over Guy's greatest strength and weakness as a CEO: He believes himself actually to have become—on a level of irony that is almost but not quite indistinguishable from reality—a True Cyberlord. When he speaks to his sales managers about their close and profitable relationship with Wal-Mart, where most of his games are sold, he tones that aspect of his personality down. Way down.

The Pornsiter

THE PORNSITER has no such pretensions to glamour. The Pornsiter is, however, an important category of yettie, one whose existence is spoken of quietly, like a Black Jack uncle you don't bring up at Thanksgiving dinner. He's a pornographer, after all, even when he's a woman, which he is, sometimes, in the Bay Area. "To his credit," says Grandmother, passing the cobbler, "there are 40,000 of these … sites out there. He's doing very well for all the competition."

The Pornsiter is rich. It is a truism of the Internet that the only Web sites that are actually profitable, the only ones that bring in substantive revenue as opposed to capital, are the ones that sell financial information and the ones that sell pornography—these are the twin deacons of the New Economy's church. The platitude discounts successful ventures like the auction site eBay, which simply introduces, at great profit, collectors of church fans to those poor souls who happen to have both Internet service and a hoard of the things in the garage, but it is nevertheless fairly accurate. In the New Economy, pornography pulls in revenues of close to $1 billion a year.

The Pornsiter has a mustache. (Some stereotypes never, ever change.) It is worn ironically, though. The Pornsiter went to Brown, where he majored in semiotics and enjoyed a fruitful series of relationships with students at the Rhode Island

(1) **Hair** like this takes an enormous amount of work, actually. The Pornsiter sneaks out of the office every other week to have it done in the privacy of his stylist's apartment, on Bank Street in the West Village. There are nine different products for its upkeep in the 10 by 12 shower-cum-steam room in his Tribeca loft.

(2) The Pornsiter's childhood next-door neighbor, who introduced him to smut in 1986, wore a **V-neck T-shirt**; he's worn one ever since.

(3) **Consignment-shop suit**, bought by an occasional girlfriend who does ironic burlesque down at Coney Island, and worn tight, tight, tight at the groin. He's in this business for a reason, after all. Only problem: He can't find a small enough mobile phone for love, money, or fucking. And he's been trying, man. It always, like, bulges wrong!

In the inside breast pocket: tickets to San Francisco from New York, tonight, and the mobile number of a hot little betty who freelances for Salon, and who just finished a piece on the Pornsiter for them. There was some serious energy going on in that interview. It's been up on the site for a week. "How do you know, as a lover, when it's okay to tie someone up?" she'd asked. She'll see. Also, the business card of a lawyer he met at a party down on Elizabeth Street, who wants to talk to him about some creative revenue dodges on the video he's selling on his site, of Britney Spears taking a leak in a Tokyo bathroom.

In the pants pocket: $107 and the wand for his PalmPilot, which he left at a betty's apartment the night before he met that lawyer, which is why the guy had to give him the card. Medeco keys to the loft. Two hits of ecstasy, wrapped in a cut-up page from *Barely Legal*. Some lint. In the back pocket: his wallet, containing a personal Chase card and a corporate charge plate from Amex. A Visa. A MasterCard. And a picture of his mom at the Jersey Shore in 1969, wearing a bikini and laughing at the camera.

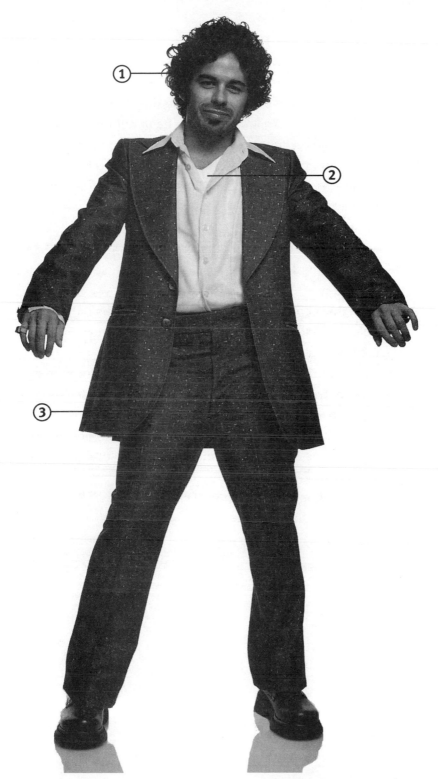

School of Design, one of whom he married, unsuccessfully for love and extremely successfully for business. While it lasted, the marriage gave the Pornsiter legitimacy; his wife was his COO. The Pornsiter claims to be enlightened in matters of human sexuality and understands, beyond his mustache and education, that there is no future in widening the interests of those who would type into a Web browser the words "fat Asians" or "teabagging" or "teen panties." He simply desires to provide the customer with what the customer desires—and at the low price of $60 a month, or $15.95 for the download of 10,000 photographs of "just-18!" amateurs. Every day.

In this aspiration, he is remarkably like his father, who runs a clothing store for large-size women in Orlando, Florida, where the Pornsiter was raised. He is 34 years old.

The Pornsiter has geek qualities; his need for better graphics and the concomitant revenue these would deliver causes him to be a firm believer in new technologies. His ex-wife, still a partner in the business, also touts technological breakthroughs as an avenue leading toward a more mainstream understanding of pornography as art.

"You'll be able to *smell* the site," she says. "Really *smell* it!" She, too, is an ironist.

THEY ARE THE STUDLIEST: CODEWRITING GEEKS AND H-1B PROGRAMMERS

YETTIES ARE A migratory species. Spend any time at all in the departure lounge at Kennedy Airport in New York, near the gates for San Francisco and San Jose, and you will see flocks of them, rafted in the low waiting chairs like ducks off the sea coast. Market corrections have had none of the effect that diminishing wetlands have had on the future of American waterfowl. As late as the summer of 2000, it was possible to observe the wide range of the yettie taxonomy just sitting there, waiting for their flights west.

You've already met some of them. There was a stone yettie CEO, for instance, reeking of Neo-Yuppie Prepster cleanliness in razor-creased khakis, pressed white buttondown, and trim blue blazer. He was flipping through *Red Herring* while he talked on a mobile phone attached to his ear. He looked about 12. There was a Mouse Jockey as well, clad in a dress-up-for-travel short black skirt with heavy-soled Steve Madden shoes and an antique cardigan sweater. She was listening to music on a small MP-3 player and reading a copy of a Chicago smart-guy zine called *The Baffler*.

There were others: assorted PR Bunnies and Salesbots, heading home to Silicon Valley HQ after a grueling few days hawking wares to East Coast dilettantes who either did or didn't want to join the hejira to *serious* bandwidth, who either did or did not in the parlance *get it*. There were a couple of Pilotfish Journalists. You'll get to know them all soon enough.

But there were a couple of programmers in the terminal as well, and entirely separately they captured the attention of a good percentage of the non–New Economists who strode past them. They seemed weirdly, counterintuitively, *important*. Programmers are like that now. They are the supergeeks, the nerdliest of the nerds: mismatched socks, eight-day jeans, nacho-stained fingers, bug-eyed glasses, a goofball mien running either to intense focus or imminent psychosis, depending on your point of view. But they also represent a strong connection to the past (the world they built, upon strings of 0s and 1s!), and they reside as a result at the intellectual center of the yettie world. Even your lowliest auto-parts sales rep, waiting at Kennedy for a flight to Las Vegas for the Carburetor 2000 convention, understands this. He knows—hey, he's read the papers—that Bill Gates was a programmer, a Nerd Made Good, a geek. Who is he to say that these fellows in the airport aren't the next Bill Gates? For the auto-parts guys, the world's turned upside down. The geeks are gods. Aren't they? They certainly could be, and most often fall into one of two yettie types.

The Codewriting Geek

THE FIRST programmer to draw attention at Kennedy that day was a Nerd Made Good with bad skin and an almost-Armani black blazer over a black T-shirt reading CHICKS DIG UNIX. He was in his late 20s, drinking a Coke and occasionally stabbing at a PalmPilot. A large computer bag lay between his feet. His hair was mussed in the manner of someone who has not only failed to shower recently but has failed entirely to sleep. It stood in greasy waves, pulled taut by the comb of his fingers. His eyes

were rimmed red under the thick glasses of a 10th-grade bio-
logy teacher, and there were food stains on both his T-shirt and
on the right lapel of his jacket. There were grease stains on his
sneakers, too, which were retro in style but not fashionably so.
His jeans were from Lee. His stomach pooched out over his belt
buckle, slightly obscuring it. He was in no manner hip.

The programmer stabbed at his PalmPilot and finished his
Coke, then went off to find another one. He returned a few seconds later to retrieve the bag that had been between his feet.
He'd forgotten it. There was the slightest hint of red in his face
then, as he looked about to see who had noticed him being a
space case, a doofus, a nerd. The auto-parts guy chuckled,
nudged his partner. "Guy's probably worth more than United,"
he said, shaking his head at the wonder of it all. "Weird."

The Codewriting Geek *is* a weird sort of yettie, and the guy
with the Cokes and the PalmPilot was a prime example of his
order. The Codewriting Geek is unlike the yetties we have met
so far in one true sense: He has never desired any sort of life
beyond the computers that have offered him succor since his
youth. The Codewriting Geek did not study East Asian reli-
gion in college. Nor did he enjoy fingerpainting in primary
school; invariably the paints spilled and the other children
laughed at him. Nor did the Codewriting Geek ever take a
year off from school to live in Maine, learning to build kayaks
and to market within a niche. Nor was he ever much of a
Deadhead or punker, nor a true Japanimation fan. He went to
college as an electrical engineer, programmed computers,
studied them, programmed some more. He's done that his
whole life. He built robots with Lego pieces as a kid, alone in
the bedroom; he made radios, built computers. He played
Dungeons & Dragons with the other nerds, rolled the dice
and dreamed, as he still does, in numbers. The Codewriting
Geek works algorithms in his head, calculating the number of

① **Eyeglasses** purchased fully a year before Patrick Naughton, who was at the time a senior executive codewriting geek at Infoseek, was accused of e-chatting up and attempting to have sex with a 13-year-old girl who was actually a full-grown police officer. Same glasses!

② **UNIX** is an operating system that originated at Bell Labs in 1969. It was a pretty important element in the development of the Internet. CHICKS DIG UNIX, says the Geek's T-shirt, and the joke of it is, of course, that that's not really true. Chicks are *much, much, much more* into the sexiness of Linux, which is a Unix derivative available in both free software and commercial versions. So the shirt's kind of funny, huh?

③ The Infernal **Mobile Phone**, which his former best friend and current CEO *makes* the Codewriting Geek wear at all times so that he can be reached with problems with the source code. At least twice a quarter the Codewriting Geek manages to "lose" the thing.

④ **Brain bag** with a Dell Inspiron 7500 in it—it's jammed with encryption software that's meant to hide the real work he's doing on it, in case some infidels from the other side try to smite him and take off with his knowledge and experience points. Also extra batteries, modem cables, a spare disk drive, and a half-eaten bag of pretzels he picked up on the way to the airport.

⑤ The Most Foul **Pager**, which is meant to be a backup for the phone. There's a woman in the front of the office whose job it is to make sure it's on and attached to his belt whenever the Codewriting Geek leaves the office. She touches him: rank pleasure and base humiliation combined.

⑥ **Jansport backpack**, containing clothes for the business trip: another pair of jeans, another pair of white socks, and two other T-shirts. One reads DON'T ASK THAT QUESTION. IT'S INCONSEQUENTIAL. The other: BUY A PENTIUM 586/90 SO YOU CAN REBOOT FASTER. Hanes Y-front underwear from Mom. Also: a toothbrush and a copy of *The Silver Call Duology* by Dennis L. McKiernan. McKiernan's no Tolkien, but it's okay.

lightposts on a certain stretch of highway, the ratio of them to hatched passing-lines on the road. He's pure in this sense: an *über*-geek. The real thing. He writes code. All else is soda runs, jerking off, and sleep.

The Codewriting Geek is possessed of valuable commodities in the yettie world. He has his talent and experience imbedded deep in his very large brain. He is known by his colleagues and the diaspora of his friends as "studly," the sort of geek who thrives on a real challenge, on the pride he gets from near impossible success. His mantra: *I can surpass the technology of any competition my employers put before me. Just give me time and space.* The Codewriting Geek programs so that his software can go from 10 users a day to 10 million. That's what he *does*, and it is, he knows, an important task.

(The New Economy was built entirely upon this keystone, by the way. Scalability. A program that does something well for one person, or a dozen people, or even 200 people at once is one thing. But the bet's on 30,000 people using it simultaneously, or 300,000. The code that supports that sort of width is exponentially more difficult to write. Here's a thought for a Codewriting Geek at three A.M. on a Wednesday four days before a company's launch. What if a million people want to access us at once? And can't? What if? He pops another Dr. Pepper, drinks deeply, and then lets his fingers drift down to the keyboard.)

The Codewriting Geek self-identifies. It's a point of pride for him. He is eccentric and proud of that fact; outside of work he'll do whatever he likes. Because he can. The New Economy is not about money for him or his friends. It's about intellectual opportunity—the chance to think.

The Codewriting Geek may live in a group house, with other Codewriting Geeks. The house he lives in may have a name: the Geekocile, for instance. There won't be many women in it. (There are women Codewriting Geeks. Not many of them. Most notable, perhaps, is Sandy Lerner, who created Cisco Systems with Len Bosack in 1984. Lerner has boasted of a terminal session in which she stayed in front of the screen for three days.) The Codewriting Geeks within the Geekocile may work for a software company but are more probably lone wolves, ready to drop any task before them for the chance to work with other studly engineers, doing what it is that they do best: write code that holds within it the possibility of changing the world.

The Geekocile will not be clean, precisely, nor will it boast any particular detailing besides piles of laundry, garbage, stuff strewn about, stacks of old hardware, creaky desks covered with new computers, large monitors, sheets of paperwork. It will, however, have serious pipe leading into it: DSL lines for every resident, so that working at home is like working at the office, wherever that may be. For the Codewriting Geek, as for many yetties, work is home, home is work.

Stock options? Codewriting Geeks may have them but are not naturally schooled in the ways of business. For a Codewriting Geek, sometimes a high hourly wage will do it. He thinks in modules. And the most important one is Quality of Challenge.

Codewriting Geeks are single. They work in bursts, for endless periods of time, without talking. They don't read much other than trade magazines, pornography, and endless screens of listserv advice and e-mail from friends. They make giddy runs to Fry's Electronics in Palo Alto to check out gear. They don't eat sushi when they order out. That nonsense is for marketing turds and "suits." Codewriting Geeks eat pizza. They eat chips. They drink endless amounts of soda. They devour Chinese. Chinese is the shit, says the Codewriting Geek. General Tso's Chicken two, three times a week, driven fast and furious from some chop-shop storefront six miles from the office park, with gelatinous sauce poured hot, sweet, and fiery over deep-fried chunks of chicken. Rice, but only a little. That's take-out, baby.

Codewriting Geeks don't tip very well. They barely remember to pay.

THE SECOND programmer at Kennedy that day was Indian, a mid-level employee of a middling-sized software company, and he sat quietly at the foot of the one public telephone in the terminal, downloading his e-mail into an extremely small laptop computer. He was wearing a turban. He had a scraggly beard. His shirt was blue denim stitched with the name of an Internet company. There were red-and-black Teva sandals upon his feet. His khakis were rumpled and ever so slightly soiled. There was a thin gold chain around his neck. And as he tapped away at his laptop in his pleated khakis and dot-com blue shirt and turban, he ate from a plastic pint of pineapple chunks and spoke into a mobile phone earplugged to his head.

This programmer cut a colorful figure there in the airport terminal. An Old Economy white businesswoman walking toward the ticket counter stopped short at the sight of him and said something to her companion, also business-rigged according to the old model. The two of them, pin-striped and uncomfortable, were lugging wheelie bags behind them.

"That says it all right there," she said, pointing with her patrician's nose. Whether there was admiration or disdain in her voice was impossible to tell, until she flipped her Suburban Career Woman bangs and moved along. But the image was clearly hard for her to shake: this programmer sitting there, calmly tapping away at his laptop attached to a pay phone and talking on a mobile phone and eating pineapple while waiting for a flight home to San Francisco. The man was somehow notable: He was a face of the New Economy. He was an H-1B Programmer yettie.

The H-1B Programmer

An H-1B is a type of visa. It is issued by the United States Immigration and Naturalization Service to allow an American company to hire a foreign programmer or engineer (any sort of professional, really, but mostly ones who work in high tech) for a period of three years. An H-1B visa can be renewed by the INS once, allowing the foreign worker a total stay of six years. It costs a couple of thousand dollars to get an H-1B, with lawyers' fees and incidentals. Which makes it a pretty sweet deal for an employer, since your man from India has generally received a better technological education than his American counterpart and, since he's foreign, you can pay him less. The median salary for American high-tech workers with less than 10 years' experience is north of $57,000. For highly-skilled and experienced H-1B visa holders—and more than 600,000 of them have come to the United States since 1990—it's more like $53,000. That's a small difference, perhaps, but small differences add up. Besides, the H-1B Programmer is dependent on his employer for his visa. He's not going to jump ship over $4,000.

But the H-1B Programmer has big dreams. The six years give him time to live them out. He is likely a graduate of the Indian Institute of Technology schools established by Prime Minister Jawaharlal Nehru in the years following the Second World War. As a prerequisite, then, the H-1B Programmer has a brilliant mind; securing a place in an IIT school is an awe-somely difficult procedure, requiring innate test-ready intelli-gence of a level that makes America's reliance on standard-ized testing as an indicator of possible future achievement look naive. In India, the Test is all there is, and the educational system there is as relentless in its adherence to its answers as it is to teaching English and computer science from the third grade. In his hometown, the H-1B Programmer recalls billboards advertising Oracle jobs, Apple computers, training in C++, and

①   Kesh is one of the five K's of Sikhism; it's the **unshorn hair** under the H-1B's turban. America's okay. There are fewer jokes about Sikhs.

②   **Dot-com denim**. The H-1B got his on the first day of his first job in the U.S.; the human-resources drone handed it to him with the non-disclosure agreement and the health-insurance packet.

③   **Water**. The H-1B is amused by the notion that the European water he drinks every day has traveled thousands upon thousands of miles— *just like him.*

④   **Brain bag**. In which the H-1B keeps his laptop—and encrypted disks full of business plans he's thinking about pitching to Kanwal Rekhi over at the Indus Entrepreneurs. Rekhi is the key to his future, thinks the H-1B. Him, and a green card.

⑤   One of the other five K's of Sikhism is the **kirpan**, or saber, with which the Sikh can fight his enemies. The H-1B's is made of plastic, and has an Intel 750 MHz microprocessor in it.

⑥   Another K! The **kara**, or steel bracelet, represents the H-1B's battle shield, and in truth he was able to use it on a business trip to Washington, D.C., when someone attempted to rob him on a side street near Union Station. The bracelet made a pleasant sound cracking into the bad man's skull.

⑦   **Travel backpack**, containing a number of New Economy magabibles, a change of clothes, a DVD for *The Matrix*, and yet another K: the H-1B's kangha, or wooden comb. (The fifth K is for "kaccha," these drawstring underpant things that the H-1B abandoned for Hanes upon his arrival in the U.S.)

⑧   **Mobile phone**, with a mike 'n' earpiece clipped into the H-1B's ear, on which he talks with friends almost every hour he is not at work coding. This amounts to one and sometimes two hours a day.

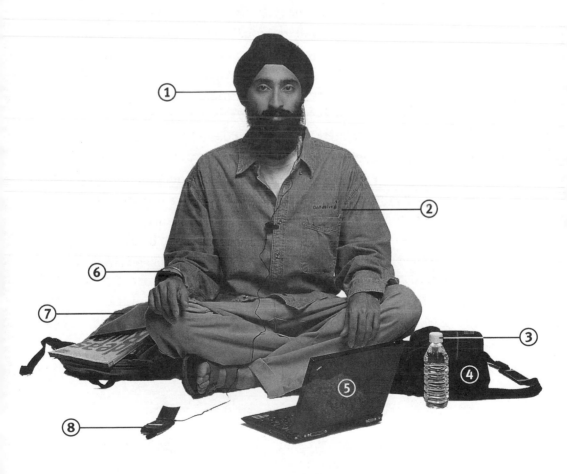

Java. These rose high above dusty streets crowded with sacred cattle, crippled children, the whole noisy bazaar of Third World life. He has prepared to come here, he says, all his life.

The H-1B Programmer is ever so slightly Anglophilic. He plays cricket in a league in Sunnyvale, California, and enjoys a strong cup of tea, brewed in a pot. He is polite, good-natured, hardworking, multilingual. Beyond English and Hindi, the H-1B Programmer speaks the local dialect of his youth and writes any number of programming languages. He likes the curry at the Santa Clara Marriott very much, and he has it whenever he attends monthly meetings of a networking group called the Indus Entrepreneurs. The H-1B Programmer has some American in him as well. He goes to these meetings hoping to grab a word with Kanwal Rekhi, a Pakistani who founded ExceLan, then sold it to Novell for $210 million. Rekhi goes to the meetings, you see. The H-1B Programmer will meet him there. He has an idea he needs to talk to Rekhi about.

Being single does not please the H-1B Programmer, though he does not voice this opinion very often. He lives in a large house one hour's drive from his job, with nine others in exactly his position in life. Each one of them has a dream, and not one of them shares it with the others. They only play cricket together, and go to the Safeway in Foster City on Saturdays, dressed in new white sneakers and crease-pressed jeans, and talk occasionally of home.

The H-1B Programmer drives a Toyota Camry. He needs a green card. He will get one damn soon.

4

IF IT SUITS THEM:
THE VC, THE BARRISTER,
AND THE CROSSOVER
GEEZER

BUCK'S RESTAURANT, which sits off Woodside Road about a mile from Interstate 280 in Silicon Valley, is a diner of the Small Town Eccentric aesthetic. Behind its plain, rural strip-mall exterior, tawny Naugahyde booths sit grandly. A large selection of eBay-friendly kitsch hangs from the ceilings, and innumerable pro-Buck's testimonials clutter every available square inch of paneled wall. Eggs any style will run you $5.00 at Buck's. The coffee's not bad.

Buck's holds a special place in the yettie cosmology. Jim Clark's Netscape IPO was hatched at Buck's. Netscape eventually went to AOL for north of $10 billion. And not just Netscape. All manner of Silicon Valley success stories—Hotmail, Kana Communication, Hopelink—have started at Buck's, the deals cut over breakfast burritos, flapjacks, toast. You can see neophytes there sometimes, pointing: *Right there at that table, Bobby. Right there!*

Buck's is not by any means an anonymous restaurant. Lazy afternoons see print and TV newsmagazines alike arriving there to "shoot" yetties in their own environment. Stylists put flab-toned venture capital boys into downmarket chic and call it fashion at Buck's; on-air talent "breakfasts" there with CEOs under klieg lighting and fuzzy boom mikes. The rest of the time, people either work deals, eat eggs, or just sit around and gawk at one another.

In weird recognition of its place in both yettie history and the public eye of the New Economy, Buck's is the business-social centerpiece of all Silicon Valley. Breakfast at Buck's can take on the import of lunch at the Grill Room of the Four Seasons or dinner at Matsuhisa, only without the tailored suit of New York or the coke-jittery arm candy of Los Angeles, respectively. Sketch out a business plan on the back of a napkin at Buck's, come back a year later with $234 million in your pocket, and word of that success (*He started at Buck's!*) will spread through the Valley like fire.

You're a yettie eating at Buck's with someone who matters in the New Economy? Pal, investor interest in your company could *soar*. Because, you know, that *is* a managing director of the largest venture capital firm in the Valley sitting in the booth by the window with a towheaded youngster armed with a laptop and a sheaf of paper that looks remarkably like a principal prospectus. What's *his* story, then? And that *is* in fact a paper-gajillionaire Valley CEO behind him, fresh off the cover of *Upside*, deep in conversation with a reporter from *The Industry Standard*. Which signifies one groundswell or another, if you're looking for one—and you should be, if you're here. And that *is* indeed a group of lawyers in the back prepping for a meeting later in the morning at Sun Microsystems. *Who for? What about?* The old lady spitting grapefruit seeds into a water glass in the middle of the room, or the dignified old coot having a 9 A.M. martini by the door—these only serve to place the yettie power-dancing in bas-relief.

You won't find many Mouse Jockey yetties at Buck's. Nor more than the occasional Nerd Made Good, explaining something complicated to a fellow with a mechanical pencil in the pocket of his Lands' End buttondown and the words LEAD UNDERWRITER virtually inked in red across his wide forehead. You will, however, find a great number of Neo-Yuppie

Prepster CEOs with Audi TT's parked in the back of the lot, away from the shade trees that might drop crap on their high-gloss wax jobs.

You will find them here in fraternity with three yettie types of great import in the New Economy's growth model. There are, first and foremost, the VC's, or venture capitalists. There are also the Barristers, to haggle contractual points and argue intellectual property rights with haughty ease. And there are the Crossover Geezers from the Old Economy, brought in to help a startup appear "mature."

The VC

THE COUNTRYSIDE WEST OF Stanford University, about 10 minutes from Buck's, begins to go dusty and starts to roll, getting ready for its ascent up into the Santa Cruz Mountains that guard Silicon Valley from the Pacific winds and fog. Yetties are thick on the ground here, and at their thickest in the anony-mous office parks that line the tarmac of Sand Hill Road. A high percentage of the world's VC funds are here, supervising something near $32 billion in capital.

For a yettie with a Big Idea, Sand Hill Road is investment Mecca; more secularly, it's Las Vegas with better odds and no-limit bets. Breakfast well at Buck's, goes the chimerical logic, and in no time flat you'll find yourself safe in a conference room at Kleiner, Perkins, Caufield & Byers signing papers that give you $20 million in seed money, for no more than 10 per-cent of the company when you take it public. Not one penny more! You play hardball here and then you go out and domi-nate the market. That, amigo, is the strategy.

Here's the thing, though. This VC? He's the most rapacious pigkiller in all of yettiedom, save a Cyberlord at his most extortionate. And then only because the VC's need for ego gratification is smaller than his desire for an unadulterated and *huge* return on his firm's investment. Venture capital used to be a gentleman's game, played by country-club duffers with long money and a keen eye for what the market would bear. They took small bets, as it were, on people they liked, and on companies that needed a jolt of capital to make it off the line into black. Stay black for a while, quarter unto quarter unto quarter unto years, and then we'll talk about going public. Maybe. It didn't come up all that often; you brought them return on profits then, more than on the IPO. It was more like a favor then. Secret handshakes and boolah-boolah club connections got you in the door: *Just don't lose us the money, old boy.*

But that, let's underline, was then. Now a VC likes a steep revenue curve, and he likes it right now. Never mind losses so much, though losses, in the waning days of the initial Internet IPO rush—and particularly since the first Nasdaq crash—are coming to bear. Beat them back with revenue. The VC likes a good, clear, path to profitability. And, by the way, it's going to be 30 percent or more of the company you'll give him to see that happen on his watch, with his money. Ten percent's a sucker's bet, and he'll laugh you right out the door.

Speaking of which, here's a yettie VC right now, caught in amber as he pushes open a door to the parking lot of a cedar-and-glass building on Sand Hill Road. He's heading out from his office to a black Mercedes with calf-leather seats and an automatic transmission. It's seven in the morning, and this VC's headed to breakfast at Buck's. He's wearing a crisp pink dress shirt opened two buttons over a concave and hairless chest, and a thin gold wedding band glints among the soft fingers of his left hand. He's tucked the shirt with military precision into pressed khaki trousers, pleated in accordance with West Coast business style, and he carries a stack of paper under his right arm. At his waist, hanging off a woven leather belt, is a small mobile Nokia phone. Black. He carries no brain bag; he has left his computer at work. His hair is sandy and thinning, his skin browned. The overall impression is that of a camp counselor on his way to Sunday chapel. Put him in a Lazard Freres banking outfit and he'd appear to be on his way to confirmation class at the local Episcopal church. He's 36 years old and hasn't been inside a bar or nightclub in over a decade.

Check out the resumé. Top of his class at Stanford. A bunch of years' programming experience with big-name software outfits, in six different computer languages. An MBA from Harvard and two years at Sun. Then straight to the firm, where he made partner in three years. The company has nearly $1 billion in committed capital and $700 million under management; it has stakes in more companies than the VC can count on his digits, and the five that went public last year had a combined market cap in the early part of 2000 of well over $1.5 billion. Down a bit from the fourth quarter of '99, but still. But still. His parents run a flower shop back home in Cleveland. He bought them their new house in Shaker Heights.

The VC has two children with his college-professor wife. He has his assistant track how many times a week he gets home to eat with them. He has her track that information *exactly*. His action-item goal is 20 times a month. This quarter he's hit 19 twice, which he thinks is pretty good and certainly better than Q4 of last year. Way better. The VC lives near his offices, in Woodside, and when he heard that the house next door to his was going to go on the market last year, he just marched right over to the owner's back door on a Sunday morning. He stood at the door in boat shoes and a faded polo shirt over his khaki shorts.

"I'll give you $4 million," he said. The house wasn't that big.

"I'll have to think about it," said the neighbor.

"I'll give you $4 million cash."

1. **Brooks Brothers dress shirt**. There's something about the feel of soft Sea Island cotton that makes the VC feel as powerful as a king in his robes.

2. **Cloth watchband**, in college colors. There's an old-boy network out there all right; real boolah-boolah, secret-handshake type stuff. It's old-school VC, that stuff, and sometimes that's exactly what you want circulating in the dealflow.

3. Should have had the goddamn gardener put the new propane tank on the grill set-up in the outdoor dining area instead of playing Mr. Handy and ending up with an **ouchie** like this.

4. **Ray-Bans**. You want some protection when you're cruising east up Sand Hill Road at dawn—not to mention that driving the 'cedes at 75 virtually demands *some* movie-star privileging.

5. Five people have the number to this **mobile phone**: two CEOs, the managing partner, the wife, and a fellow the VC's incubating on the sly, with private and personal funds, down in Cupertino.

6. A **red herring** is the term of art for a company's preliminary prospectus. It gets its name from the printed red disclaimer on the left side of the pages. If the VC says "yes" to the draft of the one he's got in this file, two fellows with bad skin and big brains are going to have a chance to make a boatload of money.

7. **Khakis**. The dictates of west-coast business-casual style demand the pleats, for which the VC takes heat when he's in New York. Pocket contents: keys to the Mercedes and $280 in cash.

8. Driving shoes from **J.P. Tod**. It's a trick the VC picked up from Barry Diller at a conference in Ketchum, Idaho, last spring: The Tods are perfect para-blasé wear for anyone who wants to convey the impression—and only the impression—of being easygoing.

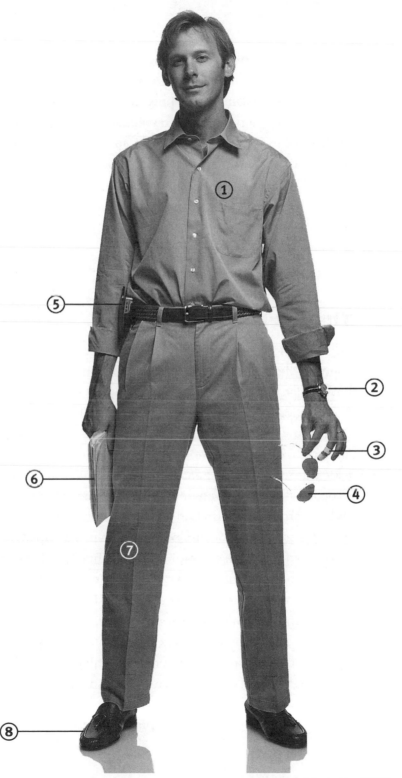

The VC has a double lot now, with a new pool and guest cottage where his neighbor's house used to be. He sits out there sometimes and thinks how one of the cool things about California, about not having to wear socks as often as you do back home in Ohio, is how the skin above his ankles hasn't yet gone hairless, as his father's did at about his age.

The VC's children ride horses at a local stable three times a week. They want their own, and the VC's thinking about it. But he doesn't like ostentatious behavior. And there's no return on a horse. They just die.

"Can we lease ponies?" he asks his wife.

The Barrister

THE BARRISTER lives up in San Francisco, in a pricey loft south of Market Street, where he keeps four mountain bikes, a Power Mac G4, a large home entertainment center, and a larger collection of dusty live-concert tapes collected at Grateful Dead shows attended religiously in college and sporadically after, right up until the moment Jerry Garcia died. Also, three wide bookcases full of dead white males and French deconstruction thereof, and an impressive number of movies on DVD. There's a platform bed on the western wall and, across from it, some edgy-looking paintings he picked up at a gallery in Manhattan's Chelsea neighborhood shortly before leaving that city to move out here to make his fortune. He's 29.

His girlfriend's cotton tank tops hang from the shower rod in the bathroom. She was a songwriter when he met her, an Oberlin grad pulling espressos for rent. Now she's organizing the city's baristas, into a union or something. Her voice is often hoarse from shouting, and she hasn't picked up her guitar since she moved into his loft. So far as the Barrister knows, anyway. They live in the same space but spend only Sunday afternoons together, riding in the hills above Berkeley. Sometimes they take the two city bikes instead of the tricked-out hillmunchers, and they go to the Mission for brunch. The Barrister suspects his girlfriend to be independently wealthy, a kind of trustafarian.

The Barrister went to Harvard Law School. The first year up there in Cambridge was grim business—it made Penn look like the long frat party it had actually been—but by L3 the Barrister was playing Ultimate every Thursday night with some buddies from the b-school across the Charles River and entertaining beaucoup job offers. He was Law Review and got high on occasional weekends. Life was just as he'd been told it would be when he was a high school lacrosse star back in Wilmington, a handsome All-American with good grades. His teachers looked on him as practically a Kennedy, then, down to the DWI bust he just barely avoided senior year. That business wasn't really his fault, they said at the time. The girl he'd been with, whose car it was—she was a troubled girl. He'd been trying to do the right thing, taking her home on that back road so late. He was destined for greatness, they said.

When he got out of law school, the Barrister took a job with the white-shoe firm in New York that had shown him big respect when he was a summer associate—paying his rent, paying for his fancy dinners with girls he'd known in college, paying him long money for short hours. They'd even paid for his New York State Bar exam prep course. The Barrister took the bar in July, then got ready for work. He went to Paul Stuart on Madison Avenue and spent $10,000 in about two hours: six suits, 12 dress shirts, nine ties, two pair of cap-toe oxfords, one pair of tasseled cordovan loafers. Then he went down to the dorm-room one-bedroom in Battery Park City that he'd rented sight unseen. And he thought, looking out the window that first night, that he might go up to Paragon

1. Under the Bobby Kennedy shirt, the Barrister wears a **tie-dyed T-shirt** he picked up at a Phish show two years ago. That had been a *jamming* show: They did a cover of "Layla" for like 20 minutes and only afterward did the Barrister find out it was a cover. Dude!

2. **City bike**. The Barrister rides it to work in the mornings even though there are a few sweat issues to deal with once he's arrived. Still, it reads right: youthful, socially aware, fit. He's asked the architect for the company's next space to put in a shower room somewhere.

3. **Fountain pen**, next to the ubiquitous mobile phone. It's a habit the Barrister picked up at the white-shoe firm, before he moved west: Gesture with a fountain pen when you're speaking in meetings and people immediately assume you know what the hell you're talking about.

4. **Persol sunglasses**. Those trolleys bust past you on Market Street, they kick up some wind, which has dust in it, which can be just hell on a man's contacts.

5. The Barrister has a **money clip** in his pocket, with three Silicon Valley food stamps wrapped around a bank card from WingspanBank.com and his Connecticut driver's license. Also keys to his Golf, his bike locks, his loft, and his office. Increasingly, he'd like to see the business of locks move to a digital application.

6. Back east recently, the Barrister went down to this place **Jack Spade** and bought a bag on the theory that every single woman he's been attracted to in the last year and a half has had a Kate Spade bag designed by this Jack fellow's wife. In it: an iBook laptop, an issue of *Wired* that has a brief interview with him in it, and the "Marketplace" section of the *Wall Street Journal*. Also, an Altoids tin containing a small wooden bat and a few buds of phenomenal Humboldt County herb, a gift from his old college roommate who's living up there and growing the stuff.

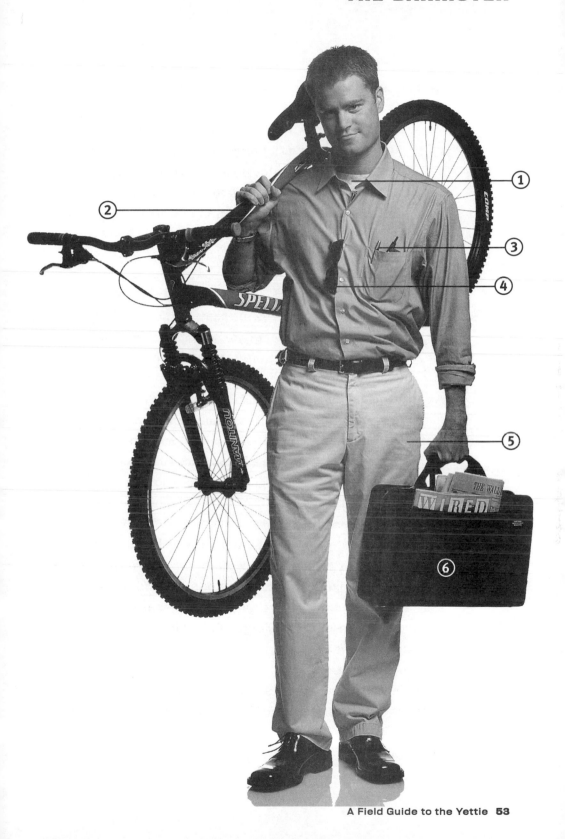

next weekend, in Union Square, buy himself some Roller-blades.

On Monday, at work, in an office about half the size of the one he'd had the previous summer, with two other first-year associates at desks beside his, the hammer came down like the hand of God himself. The Barrister had been a good law student, and he had excelled—so far as that was possible—as a summer associate. But he had never in his life been subjected to this sort of agonizing, brutal pain, this mind-numbing business of Actual Corporate Law.

"Here's a filing," a partner would say, offering an 1,100-page document. "It's basically the same sort of deal as the one we're doing with these other guys." *Basically*. First-year code for *change the names and get the thing back to me, boy*. Which is what the Barrister did at his white-shoe firm that first year. And the second. And the third. He used the search-and-replace function on his computer, and then he checked the document by hand. Commas. Document citations. Block phrases. And then again, for the closing, in a conference room that would be exactly the same as the last conference room he had been in, whether it was one in the firm's offices or one in Chicago, Paris, Detroit, London. Exactly the same. Eventually, it got to where the Barrister only knew where he was by the type of food brought in to him by the secretaries. *Croissants. Paris!* He stayed in the finest hotels in the world, and they were to him as a Motel Six might be to a drone selling cleaning supplies in the Midwest Corridor. The Ciragon Palace in Istanbul? The Barrister showered there, is all he can remember, on his way to a conference room.

Within six months there are only four words to describe the Barrister's life. Everything he knows boils down to these four words, him, a top-tenth-of-his-class Harvard Law School graduate who lives in a dorm-room one-bedroom in Battery Park

City that he sees only to change suits and pick up new shirts and ties: *long fucking billable hours.*

The Barrister makes terrific money. He needs it despite his pedigree; his law-school financial aid package was nonexistent because his father's a bank president, and the loan weight he put on was staggering. And it's not just the loans. Life is expensive when you have no time; his haircuts come at 10 at night, once a month, in his office, for $150 a pop. It's the only way. Rollerblades? After a year at the firm, the Barrister doubts he could skate a block if you spotted him the corners. He hasn't been above Chambers Street once since he started work, except for the trip to St. Vincent's when everyone thought he was having a heart attack in the middle of a closing. He was back at work later that night. He pays off the loans and pays his rent and his $10,000 credit-card note for those clothes, and he works those long fucking billable hours learning the corporate game. His checking account is bare.

Which is how, at the top of a new century, new careers are born. Those people the Barrister played Ultimate with, back in law school? The business-school ones with dark tans and goofball moneymaking schemes? By his third year as an associate, they were peppering the Barrister with almost daily hey-dude e-mails that had a simple and only faintly nerve-jangling subtext: *Come out for the Gold Rush.*

And so he did. The Barrister wrote himself a resignation letter heavy on the love for intellectual property law and bright new opportunity out west, endured hour-long conferences with partners assuring him he'd be one of them within a year—maybe three—if he only stayed, and went aboard a friend's e-widget startup for low, low money and a staggering number of stock options.

The Barrister hasn't worn a suit more than twice a week in three years, which is as good as never to him. He drives his

Jetta down to Silicon Valley three or four times a week for breakfast at Buck's and occasionally cuts west to the shoreline on the way home to smoke a joint on the beach at Pacifica and watch the surfers. He'd like to get into that one of these days. He would.

The rest of the time, to the tune of 70 hours a week—and for all his talk about the intellectual challenge of figuring out who owns what in a world in which information is like oxygen—the Barrister runs the company office. He acts as a kind of human-resources agent and chief financial officer (read, payroll officer) and house counsel and general ombudsman combined. The CEO, a 28-year-old former T-shirt salesman from the Five Towns region of Long Island with an impressive lacrosse pedigree and weirdly staggering intelligence, is at bottom kind of a flake. They've been lucky so far, the Barrister knows. But for an IPO or a buyout—and an IPO or a buyout is what they're all about—they're going to need a little help.

The Crossover Geezer

THE CROSSOVER Geezer comes to an Internet startup with a decent salary, heavy options, and a top-secret, golden-handshake deal if things don't work out within eight quarters. Because, look, the company needs him. The VC is, frankly, a little scared of going public with just the founders on board, what with their wild entrepreneurial egos and incessant craziness, fueled by attention-deficit disorder and lack of sleep. You need some gray at the temples if the company is going to blow up *huge*. The CEO who came from b-school to run a firm out of a garage in Menlo Park is *not* the one to scale up to $300 million in revenue and 520 employees over the course of a couple of years. Not in public, anyway.

"So, he's like—50? Maybe 60?" says the Barrister, introducing the idea of the Crossover Geezer to the CEO, one sunny day. The VC said something similar to the CEO just two mornings before, at Buck's, talking about the need for a "mature presence" in the offices, *someone* amid the used cubicles and dying office plants to counteract young Sarjeet the lead programmer, and the youthful Barrister, and all those T-shirted kids he hired to work 90 hours a week every week. The CEO nodded then and he nods now. Then at how smart it would be to get some full-growth timber into the board meetings, and now because, yeah, those might-have-been hippies are sometimes tough to place in the age spectrum.

"Go ahead," he says, spinning a 165-gram Frisbee on the end of his left middle finger.

"He did *incredible* work on the business side at a music label in the early '70s, and before that—*after* that? I can't remember—he was at Brown Brothers Harriman in New York. And he's my college roommate's uncle, so I got the skinny on him, above the particulars. Dude, he used to smoke pot. He knew Allen Ginsberg. That's why he moved out here! He's really into jazz, and he's got a ton of cash already. He just wants to be in the game; his daughter turned him on to e-mail in '93, and he saw the potential right away. He knows every fucking suit in San Francisco and a whole shitload in New York. Dude, he is *perfect.*"

Another nod, another few meetings, and the Crossover Geezer is aboard, with a private office, an assistant, and a mandate to do breakfast and lunch on the company at least eight times a week. *Maturity needs to schmooze* is the general message he takes home after the first week. It's a sweet deal.

The Crossover Geezer is in fact 61 years old. A year ago he walked away from his position as CEO of a middling-large brick-and-mortar retail outfit. Midlife crisis was the word on the street. He is the divorced father of three young women, the younger

① **Glasses** to connote a youth the Geezer no longer feels so keenly, bifocaled; still, he finds himself peering over them at lunch menus so much that he knows a new prescription is imminent.

② The **beard** makes up for a weak chin and some deep and recent jowling brought on, the Geezer believes, by the collapse of his marriage.

③ **Tattersall!** The kids around the office kid him for it, but the pattern makes him think of trout streams, Old Money, and Scotch: good memories.

④ The office manager gave him this **personal digital assistant** on his first day up to the office. The acronym had him chuckling, and he explained it to the woman. She looked at him very strangely then, and he let the matter drop. He takes it out occasionally, but the type is exceedingly small, and the whole business of writing things on it with the stick is too frustrating to bear.

⑤ A shoulder bag from **Coach**, which in the world the Geezer comes from connotes high creative intelligence: Book editors and closeted poets down at the firm had them. In it: a copy of his contract with the startup, which he'd had negotiated by his man at Thatcher, Simpson in New York. It's ironclad; he'll have $2 million in the account by Q4 2002, no matter what happens in the market. Also, a Zagat restaurant guide for San Francisco, sheaves of credit-card receipts from breakfasts, lunches, dinners, and putatively samizdat versions of the company's red herring.

⑥ The Crossover Geezer always, always wears the **waist of his pants** high, as if to prepare for Florida breezes, golf in the mornings, early-bird specials, endless nighttime trips to the john. He's getting old.

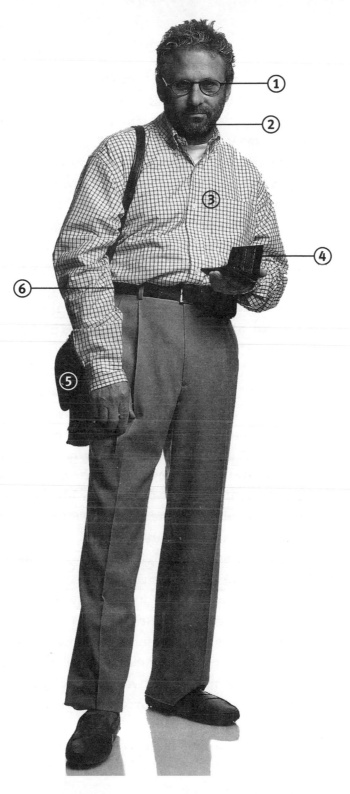

two of whom are stone yetties: One's a market analyst for a Manhattan Internet startup that tracks IPOs for online investors; and the other's a PR Bunny for a large-going-larger software outfit in the Valley. The oldest girl's married and raising kids in Vermont; her husband sold his software company to Microsoft two years ago for $110 million and now runs an organic dairy farm that operates at only a slight loss. The geezer's ex-wife is up there, too. She ashramed in the '70s and now owns a crafts store in Manchester Center. She lives with a guy who runs the snowmaking operations at one of those icy East Coast ski hills.

The Crossover Geezer has only smoked pot five, maybe six times in his life. His tastes run to tattersall shirts and wheat-colored corduroys. He did in fact cut his business teeth at Brown Brothers and had indeed left after five years to work at a record label a friend from Williams started after the counter-culture hit big. But he cut ties with the place after eight months—"freaks," he thought, privately, was indeed the apposite word for those he'd encountered—and returned to the wide halls of the Old Economy. The hippie stint helped him enormously there, however; he seemed perpetually to be the go-to meeting guy, the worldly one with the new way of look-ing at things. By 1978, the nascent Geezer was comfortably running a retail sporting-goods demi-empire and watching his marriage deteriorate. In 1980, his company moved to the West Coast. He took the children and went.

The Crossover Geezer drives a Volvo Cross Country wagon; it makes him feel young. He lives in a faux colonial house in Atherton with a real den, and he'll throw barbecue parties in the summer for the kids at the office, who will treat the Saturday afternoons in his well-groomed yard exactly as his own children do, which is to say with a mixture of nostalgia and contempt. He will golf no fewer than four times a month. Soon, the Crossover Geezer will commence a sexual relationship with one of the women in his new company's marketing department; she will be his eldest daughter's elder by 14 months.

But the road to the IPO—how much smoother it will roll beneath the feet of the CEO and the VC and the Barrister and the H-1B Programmers and all the rest! For with this firmspun old codger in among them, chairing meetings and keeping people on message and away from the whiteboards, with his encyclopedic knowledge of Old Economy gurus and his apparently limitless capacity for bullshitting it with tales of future profits and brilliant models for revenue growth, how can the company fail? The Crossover Geezer will be the king of the road show—when the company takes its act to investors the country wide, courting interest in its IPO—and he will make sure ("Goddamn fucking sure," he says over a cheeseburger at Buck's one day) that all will go well.

The Crossover Geezer is equal parts mascot and father figure and Trojan horse. He is a yettie, of course, but in the most abstract sense. He is a human security blanket.

5

TO MARKET, TO MARKET: SALESBOTS, MARKETING GEEKS, BIZ-DEVS, AND PR BUNNIES

HERE'S A FUNNY thing about yetties. They don't really talk very much—when they're running their whole New Economy jive on Mom and Dad and the fatty young Pilotfish at news outlets who reify them and make books like this one possible— about the granite cornerstone of the culture they've made for themselves: sales. Talking to yetties about yetties, you hear a lot about big brains. You hear a lot about killer applications that can invent—and then dominate—a market on the strength of a simple, brilliant idea. You hear about hits, which are the number of people who visit a particular Web site or page in a given hour, or day, or week. You hear disjointed conversation after caffeine-addled rant about stock options and company growth and market share and projected revenues and bandwidth and wealth. Not money, but *wealth*.

But you hear almost nothing about sales. And even less about the poor schmucko Salesbot who has to drive into an office park off Route 128 in the Boston suburbs at seven in the morning to make a sales call with a piece of software that the geeks have only 80 percent finished. He needs to sell 50 seats worth of that unfinished software at $300 a pop today—that is to say, he needs to acquire 50 paid users from this company off Route 128 *right now,* this morning—in order to make his quarterly sales projection. Yetties don't speak about that guy much at all.

Which is not to say that yetties don't talk about the market for their wares. You do hear, in the field, a lot of stories about the testosterone-fueled slickboys who, as the Biz-Devs of business development, combine marketing logic with a CEO's drive for investors, in order to position their company in the right spot for an IPO or a stock split or a buyout. And you also hear tales about PR Bunnies, with their endless parties and limitless supply of freebie mouse pads and perpetual off-the-record flirt sessions with tech reporters—all of it to help make sure a company increases or at least maintains its profile in the popular consciousness. Likewise, if you flip through some of the advertising-fat yettie magabibles like *Fast Company* and *Red Herring,* you'll see (as you will later in this chapter) ink devoted to Marketing Geeks, who are the fellows who figure out how to place a company in the sales arena in precisely such a way as to make consumers think solely of Oaktrees.com when they're thinking of buying a shade tree for the yard. But on your own— eating a to-go mesclun salad in San Francisco's South Park, for instance, or having an afternoon coffee at Café Gitane, a short grounder from Silicon Alley in Manhattan—you won't hear much about actual, you-gonna-buy-the-thing? sales, and in any look at how things are sold in the New Economy agora, it's important to begin with those who perform that task.

There is an important reason for the relative silence in yettie culture about those who sell product instead of ideas. It has much to do with snobbery. More precisely, it has to do with a widely held yettie belief in the hoary old cliché that is revenge of the nerds. Yettie culture reveres intelligence above all other qualities. The yettie liturgy would have it that the New Economy is a hierarchy of pure and unadulterated smarts, and that the success of any given company within that hierarchy is the result of the technological advances put forth by its brilliant engineers and designers, and to a sometimes greater extent by the deal-making genius of the corporate smart-guys.

People who make sales calls simply don't fit into that hierarchy. They couldn't! Salesmen, after all, are the dumb jocks who played football in high school and mocked the unbeautiful mathletes who took advanced-placement classes. They're the sweet-talking assholes in college who played golf and went out with sorority sisters. They're every dumb-cluck jerkoff a geek yettie has ever had to face in his life—and now they work on the next floor down struggling to under-stand a product a geek built, so that they can take it on field calls. Yetties barely consider salesmen human beings. Salesbots, they call them, for the robotic computer program inside a Web page that can take orders from interested view-ers, just as a human might have, over the phone, in the Old Economy.

A similar sort of contempt plagues Marketing Geeks, Biz-Devs, and PR Bunnies, and for similar, and similarly inaccurate, reasons. But before we get to them, let's visit with the most beleaguered yettie of all.

The Salesbot

THE DIVIDE between high-yettie geeks and shoe-leather high-tech salesmen is not simply one of intelligence—nor, more accurately, of *perceived* intelligence (there are plenty of intensely bright Salesbots, after all, just as there are plenty of rock-stupid programmers). It is instead one of motivation. Salesbots are not generally motivated by a desire to be on the cutting edge of technological development, nor are they driv-en by intellectual challenge. They're not motivated by love of system architecture. Nor are they devoted to the technocracy that Codewriting Geeks dreamed about when they were coding primitive role-playing games to replace the pencil, paper, and dice of the Dungeons & Dragons games that sustained them through junior high. As a Salesbot might say, that shit doesn't matter.

No, what matters to the Salesbot is money. For a Salesbot, money is the whole and complete thing. Not stock, nor options, nor promissory notes—only money itself. W-2 money, as it's called in the fields of Silicon Valley. "I like a *fat* stack of money in my bedside table," a Salesbot told me once in San Francisco, on his third or fourth Amaretto-and-Sprite, employing a classic Salesbot technique of mixing superannuated pop-culture references to explain a point. "I like the smell of money in the morning. I like to wake up and show me the money."

Nerds Made Good, Mouse Jockeys, even Neo-Yuppie Prepsters, will tell you that those in the sales department of their company have very little to do with them, that Salesbots aren't really yetties at all, that they're just high-tech rug merchants. Incorrect, you Jolt-fueled and greasy-haired technicians, you discreetly tattooed English majors with rope-like deltoids and weekend Ultimate games! A Salesbot *is* a yettie, albeit a yettie of the most curious sort: an old-school striver who has tasted the Kool-Aid of the New Economy and found it addictively flavorful. A Salesbot understands perhaps better than any other yettie save the Marketing Geek that the new, new thing his engineer CEO came up with in a daydream, which scored $25 million in seed capital and a force of brilliant Codewriting Geeks to make it grow, is or will be at bottom a *product*. And that without someone to sell that product to the market it will remain sitting there on a shelf in the middle of cyberspace, untouched. A Salesbot knows that the point of the New Economy is, at bottom, exactly the same as the point of the Old one: *You have to move the units.*

①   Does he **shave?** Like some freaking 1950s Dagwood character, you mean? The Salesbot spends his time with people in the *trenches*, selling to people who *understand*. And those people don't have *time* to shave. He doesn't, either, except when it's necessary. And even then, the sideburns are a righteous bohemian hedge.

②   The **mobile**'s a lifeline; he logs thousands of minutes a month on the thing. Everything's phone, except for when he's closing the deal itself.

③   The **PDA**'s a lifeline, too; it's got pretty much every single piece of useful information from the office PC on it, and his schedule, and more detailed versions of all the numbers he has programmed into the phone. Man, if they had a PDA phone the size of a stick of Wrigley's the Salesbot could sell it with his mouth taped shut.

④   The suit, the shoes, the socks, the boxers, the bag—the Salesbot is **Bananarepublic.com** from head to spit-shined toe. He hits the bookmark and orders new gear probably once a month. Sometimes twice when he hits his sales goals early. In the bag: a *Boston Herald* opened up to the sports section; copies of the software he's selling and the "literature" that heralds its perfection for cross-market application; a few business magazines; and a three-pack of Trojan rubbers, because he never has time to go home before dates and never brings women home to his apartment, and he's just being careful, okay?

⑤   The **cheapest street sunglasses** available on Route 128. The Salesbot loses or breaks on average four pairs a month, generally by sitting on them when he gets back to the car after a shitty sales call.

The Salesbot grew up in western Massachusetts, the son of a nurse. He's been messing around with computers since he was in the fifth grade, got through high school on attitude, luck, and Internet-scammed term papers, then spent the entirety of his otherwise disastrous college career in Boston flipping cheaply purchased PalmPilots onto eBay for net profits of around $75 a shot. He used the cash to pay his way through school. He's working for a software startup now, down in the flats of lower Cambridge, near MIT. He sells, out of a three-year-old Nissan Maxima that serves as his mobile office, a setup that automates your company's accounts-receivable process. "Let's say you're selling bulk Beanie Babies," the Salesbot says. "Does Mr. Toy Store wait a month for his Beanies? No, he does not. So why should you wait for his money? Because you have paperwork piled up a mile high in AR? Forget it. Invoice says pay up in 30 days? Time was it was 50 before you knew it. I can make that a goddamn *memory*."

The Salesbot wears a suit from Banana Republic, three-buttoned, stained at the lap and lapels with food grease. Scuffed Kenneth Cole loafers with large stainless buckles on them. His white dress shirt is, at the end of the day, rumpled and pulling out of his waistband, near where his Nokia mobile is clipped; he keeps the earpiece rig for it jammed into the inside breast pocket of his jacket. He's forever pushing his shirttails back in; this is a Salesbot tic observable in almost every city in the United States. His hair is sandy; it offers an unfortunate dusting of dandruff to his shoulders. There's a copy of Sun Tzu's *The Art of War* in his messenger bag, along with *Red Herring*, a *Boston Herald* opened to the sports pages, some envelopes from the online broker Ameritrade, a Palm V, and a stack of literature that explains just what it is that his company's product can do for your bottom line. The Salesbot smokes Marlboro Lights furiously, and his knee bounces up and down as if to keep time with a hummingbird's heart rate. In conversation, though, the jiggling stops, and he looks so deeply into the eyes of his interlocutor that it's disarming, as if his job were to hear confessions as much as to sell.

"You got it, baby," the Salesbot says. "Listening is half the game right there. Builds trust." And the other half? "*Closing the deals*. I read somewhere where some Valley guy said the Internet economy is an ideas economy. But from where I stand, that's just fucking bullshit. I don't sell ideas. I sell bottom-line results. You just give me my quota, and 3X commission after I hit it. That's all I need."

Tomorrow the Salesbot's cold-calling companies in the region where he grew up. He wants to have a Lexus SUV by Q4 2000, and the Berkshires are going to serve it up to him. "They still use abacuses out there," he says with a grin. "My man, I am gonna come to them like Jesus Christ himself."

The Marketing Geek

IT'S AN ARTICLE of faith in many sectors of the yettie business culture that the best technology will take the day. Until, of course, even better technology takes the market. Until better technology still alters the market and wins for itself. Unto the quarters. Vertical growth.

The Marketing Geek knows that tenet to be false. More accurate, she thinks, is the doctrine that says better technology is a *given*. It's where these companies come from, after all, rising like a covey of quail out of the fevered minds of entrepreneurial Codewriting Geeks who believe most strenuously in their killer apps and faster whatsits. That someone somewhere has come up with a better technology than the stuff that already exists means only that he can tap out a one-page business plan and garner some seed capital and begin to hire a staff.

① **Tortoiseshell glasses** from Oliver Peoples. They add, the Marketing Geek thinks, about 25 IQ points to her appearance. Not that she needs them, no.

② A single-diamond **Tiffany's pendant** her father gave her the morning she graduated from college, which is the last time she remembers crying about anything at all.

③ If you work in Silicon Valley, and you're up and down from San Francisco all the time, you become all about the **sweater set**. It's the only way to deal with the temperature changes. Cashmere, of course. So comfortable.

④ **Sporty watch!** Her yoga instructor got one from Japan six months before you could get them in the Valley; she e-mailed a friend there and had one on her wrist the very next time she went to class.

⑤ **Capris** are going to pass from fashion soon, and the Marketing Geek loves them so much she's virally-testing the notion of renaming the things "banjo pants" and citing subtle differences between them and capris in order to keep them au courant and therefore an acceptable part of her wardrobe.

⑥ Bag from **Liz Claiborne**, and all she carries to meetings now. There's something counter-intuitive and cool about marketing laptop-free, she feels. And it sets off her phone nicely: Old Economy meets New.

⑦ **Prada!** The Marketing Geek likes just *saying* that word. Let the rest of the Valley wear clunky workboot shoes; she slides that toggle down onto the top of her shoe and feels as if she's already married to the CEO.

It does not mean, not in any substantive way, that better technology will win. It means only that better technology has a chance.

No, says the Marketing Geek, it is *marketing* that brings success in the New Economy. Every time. "You think the feds went after Microsoft because their products are just so much *better* than everyone else's?" she asks. "That Microsoft was predatory toward its competitors because their operating system is a *better* operating system than the Mac OS, or Linux?" The Marketing Geek's laughing now. Marketing at Microsoft would be a terrific gig, she thinks, even today. "You know why so many people use Microsoft products?" she says. "Because *so many people use Microsoft products.* It's that simple."

The Marketing Geek used to work for a Web-design firm in San Francisco. That place pissed her off. They didn't listen, and they weren't going anywhere revenue-wise, and she didn't really fit into the culture at all, what with all its guerrilla street-marketing crap tactics. Everyone on Potrero Hill knew the name of the place, but no one knew what they did. It was like the Pets.com of Web-design firms, the Marketing Geek says, adding that this was through no fault of her own. Everyone *loved* their company mascot and their name and their tagline, but no goddamn business ever came through the door. The Pets.com sock puppet began to give the Marketing Geek nightmares. She got out six months ago, and fast. Moved down to a tiny place in Palo Alto that costs her a third more than her place in the Mission. It's lonely down there, sometimes. Everyone's Stanford where she lives, or VC and kind of invisible, except at the supermarket.

The Marketing Geek is 28 years old, with an MBA from Wharton and a small tattoo of a shooting star on her upper right biceps. She's three laser appointments from getting the thing erased entirely, which is more than she can say about the night she got it, in love with some band boy from Chattanooga she'd thought about trying to manage. He'd gotten the same tattoo, and then three nights later ditched her in a bar. The Marketing Geek works at a hardware company in San Jose now. She came on with 20,000 stock options, to be vested over four years in equal amounts. She's nearly a year in; she'll get $1/4$ then, and $1/36$ each month thereafter for the remaining three years. There's a stock-purchase plan as well, and a 401(k) for the losers who don't play the market hard. There's health, dental. It's awesome. She figures her options at nearly $100,000 now, with huge potential to rise—barring, that is, another stock market disaster and the rollbacks it would cause.

The Marketing Geek is really into cashmere sweater sets; a conservative little cardigan with beaded stitching is just the thing for half her meetings, while the tight little number underneath it works best for the other 50 percent. Also capri pants. When it comes to pants, she's like a walking advertisement for the Gap. And *very* fashionable shoes, which she suspects is how she got that terrible job on Potrero Hill. They saw the shoes and figured her for a hipster. She's not a hipster. Hipsters are lame.

The Marketing Geek drives a leased Saab convertible to work every morning, and to the San Jose airport when she travels, which is a lot. She likes to think in the car, listening to Moby, running a quadraform mental attack on the product her company's developing, which she has to market: first conception, then pricing, then promotion, then distribution, over and over again. Occasionally she calls in to the office—her mobile's hooked into the cigarette lighter, and there's a microphone clipped to her sun visor—and spits her thoughts out to someone on her team. She does the same thing at three in the morning, via e-mail, typing in bed. She's all about ideas.

On the seat next to her is a bag the Marketing Geek picked

up at a networking conference she attended last year. In it is her laptop and her Palm, a vial of the sandalwood oil she swears by as a beauty essential, and a large bottle of Fiji water. Also some Neruda poems that a girlfriend from Colby sent her last month from Amazon as a birthday gift. She hasn't gotten around to reading them yet.

A beater Volvo passes the Marketing Geek on the right and then bombs into an exit ramp for the 237, probably bound for Milpitas, somewhere like that. There's an old bumper sticker on its stern, stuck amid calls for the visualization of whirled peas and the immediate end to domestic violence, and it reads MACINTOSH 89 = WINDOWS 95. The sticker sends the Marketing Geek into a paroxysm of laughter.

"Whatever!" she yells at the Volvo. That's her point exactly.

The Biz-Dev

OUR MAN in business development is a soi-disant "safe black guy" from suburban Maryland, who majored in history at Wesleyan. He has worked at nine different Manhattan Internet startups over the course of the past six years. He has never been fired from a position; he has always quit on the promise of better chances elsewhere. Nevertheless, he says, with calm authority and only the very slightest hint of the mattress sales-man in his voice, he learned a *lot* at each place, even when the jobs weren't successful. Most important, he says, shooting his cuffs from within a Hugo Boss summer-weight suitcoat, "Keep moving. Like a shark, you know?"

Like a Biz-Dev! Business development is the realm of the slickest yetties, the ones who wear their suits on the outside like the Old Economy masters, and who find themselves equally at home amid Paul Stuarted bankers and Web-designing hot girls in baby-tees marked PERVERT. Business development isn't marketing, you know. It's not close to that. It's about *deals*. The Biz-Dev specializes in second-round VC financing, in partnering with other startups to the exclusive traffic-profit of his own, in assessing the pros and cons of changing the tack of the business plan, and in regularly perpetuating the notion that Things Could Be Better Around Here. Biz dev is about one thing, the Biz-Dev says: *Monetize the brilliance.* The Biz-Dev has been on Silicon Alley since its baby-step days, you understand, 75 hours a week minimum; he's been inside more shops than his CEO even knows exist. The message is: He knows what works and what doesn't. With him around, he makes pains to argue, there's no need for consultants. The Biz-Dev is the consultant.

The Biz-Dev knows that the suits he wears—Boss, Beau Brummel, one Armani—help underscore this image. He's almost like the Banana Republicans, but with upgrades: the suit itself, then agnès b. shirts, shoes by Varda. He has heavy debt outstanding on his MasterCard to pay for all that. But the clothes are *necessary*, he says. He knows that they bother some of the programmers at the shop where he works, a large loft crammed with polished stainless-steel desks and gleaming new iMacs. But so what if biz dev in Silicon Valley runs to pleated Brooks Brothers khakis and neat light-blue buttondowns? This is New York, for one thing. And for another, the Biz-Dev knows his color throws a good vibe into the air— makes him, to these brainy little whiteboys from Dallas and St. Louis and Scarsdale, yet another example of the boatraising power of the Web. The Biz-Dev, in his suit, is smart like that. What he likes: The kids at his job just don't know quite what to make of him, heading off to VC meetings at Draper Jurvetson's new Manhattan branch, to content-play meetings in wide Spring Street lofts, to dinner at Odeon with short-film impresarios and we-sell-e-art hucksters, to drinks with a frat

1. Not that the Biz-Dev would wear **Van Heusen!** But the Reege made it okay for folks just to look *sharp*: The Biz-Dev loves the tone-on-tone urban outfitting.

2. Beats on the **Sony VAIO** music clip: Lil' Kim rapping freestyle mixed with some world beat mixed with a DJ Spooky mix mixed with a Gilles Peterson mix mixed with some live Hootie. The Biz-Dev is Mr. Napster when he's sitting up in the office late night and bored.

3. The Biz-Dev checks his **voice mail** at work, at home, and on the mobile with the alacrity of someone eager to hear about the birth of a sibling's child. There's business coming his way, is his feeling. He's not going to miss it.

4. **Spoon watch**. He's got some creative in him after all!

5. The bag's by **Prada**. The reading material's by *Wired* and *The New York Times*, which the Biz-Dev reads religiously on the subway from Fort Greene because that's what you do if you're a successful New Yorker heading to work. He's not pulling out the *Daily News* like some back-office clown, not in this lifetime. He'll read that shit on the can. Also in there: a Sony SuperSlim Pro Notebook laptop, which weighs less than four pounds, a tube of Aquafresh toothpaste for his desk at the office, the keys to his apartment, and a crumpled credit-card receipt from the bar in the front of Junior's Restaurant on Flatbush Avenue Extension in Brooklyn, where the Biz-Dev somehow managed to spend $237 on a Friday night three months ago. He's still puzzling that one out.

buddy from Morgan Stanley, to some sort of dance club in East Flatbush on Saturday night. They just don't know, except that he brings in the deals.

And the Biz-Dev likes it that way. His computer experience boils down to a successfully completed series of programs in the computer lab back in high school and a hell of a lot of what he still calls Web surfing in college. And now this, these past six years. He's *in*. "These people don't hire for business development because they *want* to," the Biz-Dev says. "They need to. That's huge."

The Biz-Dev lives in a floor-through apartment in Fort Greene, just two stops on the D from Broadway-Lafayette. It's filled with plants he's hired a woman down the block to water and a sizable portion of the Williams Sonoma inventory, most of it shining and new; he eats out, sushi in Manhattan, six nights a week, usually after 10 P.M. There are cotton-weave rugs on the floor, Ikea furniture above it, a big TV, and a workstation with a company-leased iMac on it that he hardly uses except for e-mail and to run music through to Bose speakers his mother bought him when he got out of school. He's had precisely one woman in there since he got the place two and a half years ago for $1,100 a month. He can't remember her name.

The Biz-Dev has a mountain bike in there, too, a Cannondale he bought to ride in the woods of Prospect Park every morning he can. That's twice a month, give or take a day. He comes across all kinds of wild-ass shit out there in the park, things straight out of a New York the *Times* tells him is gone now, that only happens in movies: crazy blow-job hookups in the trees above Grand Army Plaza, pop-eyed Dominicans cutting up chickens amid candles and drumbeats way up on Santeria Hill, down by the lake. That's the real world, the Biz-Dev thinks, riding. And as nice and real as it is to see, it'll be nicer still to *remember*, when he gets his four-bedroom Victorian in South Orange, Jersey-style.

Thus work. There's a file cabinet in his bedroom, under a corn plant that grows high against the window, in which he keeps the paperwork outlining his option package at work, should he break with principle and stay for a year. He looks at it sometimes, and at the files behind it that outline the deals he's had before. They can make him smile, get him ready for a day on the street. He is ready, he says, for big-time success.

The Biz-Dev carries a shoulder bag from Prada and has in it a copy of the latest *Industry Standard*. Also David J. Gladstone's *Venture Capital Handbook*, which he reads on the train, and a Cassiopeia E-100 personal digital assistant. Every contact he's ever made in New York City, San Francisco, San Jose, Los Angeles, and Chicago is on it. Every meeting he's had. Every one he will have. Everything. Women, too, numbers for pretty little PR Bunnies and content-providing ex-*Voice* interns and self-serious *Essence* researchers and old college flames, all there and updated constantly though he hasn't had a date in six months—no time. The PDA he gives his PDA is infectious; he's had seven friends switch from Palm to the Cassiopeia as a result, and there's a note about that in the machine to celebrate it: "Explore poss. of working for Cass." Headphones from a Sony MD MZ E-60 snake out of the Prada on a wire; he's got downloaded Jay-Z on it, again for the ride to work, New York beats to make the Biz-Dev smile.

On the corner, near the train, the Biz-Dev shoots his cuffs again, checks the time on his Spoon watch. He's got an 8:30 in Tribeca to discuss an online menu service with some friends from Wesleyan. It could be his next gig, he says, if they have the money and the smarts to let him run the road show and, after that, the business end of the business itself. The Biz-Dev, after six years, is getting sick of offering advice, taking home salary. He's got those suits to pay for and that dream house to buy. You know what? It's getting to be time to move on.

The PR Bunny

THERE IS, in San Francisco just now, a small public relations firm called Marino Inc. run by three young sisters called Susie Marino, Marianna Marino, and Andrea Marino-Bodin. Their clients run to Apple Computer, Hewlett-Packard, Yahoo!, and a bunch of high-wire Internet startups eager for notice and increased market share. Marino Inc. has been in business since 1994, which in the weird time-warp calculus that is "Internet time" means that it has been around virtually forever. It is as white-shoe an Internet public relations firm as any yettie CEO or journalist is likely to find.

As happens a little more than occasionally in the public-relations sphere, at least when the flacks are female, the Marinos are fetching in appearance. (If they had been born male, fate and good fortune would have deeded them fatness, a broad sense of humor, and playfully beady little eyes.) So when in the spring of 2000 the fashion magazine *Harper's Bazaar* decided to devote an issue to this fabulous new dot.com thing that was going on in America, and it sent a writer named Nancy Jo Sales out to San Francisco to talk to people about the prospects for women who wanted to marry multimillionaire yettie CEOs, it was natural that the Marino sisters came up in more than a few conversations. Susie Marino, one source told Sales, is "the prettiest girl who'll ever look at me." (He was a source, rather than a name, because apparently he'd gone out with Marino once.)

In New York City, that sort of line would rate Marino fairly low on the ladder of professional importance—down there with cocktail waitresses at a boite in the meat-packing district, perhaps, or coatcheck girls at a Soho nightclub. But in the high-tech world, where men outnumber women by a ratio of around seven to three, it makes her kind of a star in whose shadow young publicists hop and hop. PR Bunnies, the yettie CEOs call these women, right before handing them accounts upon which a stock price may soar or crater, depending on the publicity. To the women themselves, this paradox is sort of hilarious.

And here's one now, an archetype PR Bunny of middling rank, standing guard near the door of an airy downtown San Francisco loft. She had come to the party well in advance of her clients and has been standing at her post by the door, beaming, for the better part of an hour, greeting guests. The PR Bunny wears a fitted, dark denim jacket over a dressy tank top that does little to hide the outline of her high breasts, and Marc Jacob slacks over three-inch Gucci slides she'd purchased online one afternoon last week, for stress relief. Her blond hair falls onto her shoulders in the style of a TV comedienne: Jenna Elfman, say, or Tea Leoni. The PR Bunny shakes her mane sporadically and greets each arriving person she knows (roughly 80 percent of the invited list) by name, exactly in the manner of a flirtatious politician. She offers each of those she knows with anything more than passing recognition a warm and friendly hug. People she has been to lunch with, for instance.

Later, the PR Bunny will approach each of those guests she needs to spin—a journalist from one of the magabibles about a second-round financing snafu at the shop for which the party is being thrown, for instance—and get that person a drink, or more pieces of sushi, or an extra gift bag, and eventually, off in a corner, as if she had all the time in the world, she will extract whatever it is she needs from him. A promise,

① **Gucci sunglasses** as hair band: casual and spendy both!

② Don't you just *love* the **scarf**?

③ **Kate Spade bag** containing the latest *Harper's Bazaar*, a PalmPilot, a 23-page list of invitees to tonight's party, Kiehl's #1 lip balm, Kiehl's SPF 30 sunscreen moisturizer, a tube of MAC lipstick, water (three quarts a day!), an extra battery for the mobile, three scrunchies, nine paper clips, a Santana ticket stub. Her wallet's on the passenger seat of her Jetta, out in the lot. The most valuable thing in it, to the PR Bunny's subconscious mind, is the photograph of her boyfriend from college, with whom she broke things off for no reason she can articulate.

④ "Look at this **phone**, sweetie. With it, I can get you the quote you need. So play very, very nice and don't ask me out again."

⑤ You can go short-short with the **skirt** sometimes, but it's a fool's game if you're working a room as a host, because you can't ever really tell when you're going to have to start pulling boxes around, or loading Chardonnay into the ice buckets.

⑥ Three-inch **Gucci pumps**, purchased in a spasm of retail therapy a week and a half ago. There are some women who would perch in these as a man caught on the ledge of a building in a hurricane might stand. The PR Bunny is not one of these women. Still, she'll drive home barefoot later this evening and feel a rush of pleasure in the wake of the pain that will rival but not exceed a low-level orgasm.

usually. A promise disguised as a favor returned off a favor, with the understanding that in receiving the promise-cum-favor, the PR Bunny is in fact doing the mark (as she thinks of journalists, generally) a favor, and not the other way around. She will do this perhaps 16 times over the course of the party, to 16 different individuals, for results both picayune and gigantic. It is exhausting work, and her shoes will start to kill her at about hour 1.5 of the party, but this is in great measure her job, and she enjoys it immensely.

The PR Bunny lives in the Presidio, in an insulated yettie demimonde apartment that until recently she shared with two other girls in her firm. She is six years out of the University of California at Santa Barbara and retains the flat stomach and fit legs of the recreational surfer she was during her time there. She majored in communications and minored in athlete boys, and began reading Trollope during her senior year for no reason that she can adequately explain. One of his novels was there in the library one day, and she just, you know, picked it up. And that was that. She *just* finished the last one, one novel after another, a chapter a night no matter how tired she got—which was very.

The PR Bunny is really into yoga. She goes to class twice a week, during the day, before things at the office get out of hand. She drives a '94 Volkswagen Jetta, used, that she bought off a product manager who soured on the Web when his company went public and saw its stock price head straight to the gutter. Last the PR Bunny heard, the product manager was working as a personal trainer in Bel Air, about 10 blocks from where the PR Bunny grew up, the only daughter in a family of boys. Her mom's a social worker. Her dad's a network executive, someone most people have never heard of, especially in San Francisco.

The PR Bunny doesn't have time for a boyfriend now and

thinks that having one would be a liability anyway; boyfriends
lead to marriage, and a ring on her finger would take away
one of her most successful PR techniques, which is to schedule, with an important mark, the Late Drink. She loves her job.
"It's much easier to be successful out here," the PR Bunny
says, "when people think you're dumb, easy, and hot."

6

MOUSE JOCKEYS: WELCOME TO THE CUBE FARM

IN 1993, a journalist named Paul Saffo contributed an essay to *Wired* magazine in which he made the argument that cyberpunks, those proto-yettie hacker kids born out of the imagination of novelists like William Gibson and brought to life on the Internet, should be compared most closely to beatniks, those free-expression 50s poets and novelists and jazzmen whose berets and curling cigarette smoke prefigured the hippies of the 1960s. The beatniks, Saffo argued, had been harbingers of a broader cultural elite—and the cyberpunks should be seen in the same light.

The existence of cyberpunks portended the imminent arrival of a mass movement of high-tech hipsters, Saffo asserted, who would transform the world as surely as the hippies did in the wake of Jack Kerouac and Allen Ginsberg. "Once labeled," he wrote of beatniks and cyberpunks, "both movements quickly surrendered their visual archetypes to the cultural mainstream."

Yetties didn't properly surface until the dawn of the 21st century, of course. But surface they did, en masse, bringing with them a great deal more than the cyberpunk's "visual archetype." William Gibson's watershed 1984 novel *Neuromancer* (which was, for what it's worth, typed on a 1927 Hermes typewriter, seven years before the launch of Tim Berners-Lee's World Wide Web) helped initiate a particular notion of cyberspace in the popular imagination, one of great opportunity, palpable risk, and excitement. Yetties have drawn on that memory to the exclusion of almost all other cultural stimuli save the free market. As a result, the notion of the Internet as an alternate universe—as a freewheeling and gigantic "space" as opposed to the banal "information superhighway" described by politicians and parents and well-meaning librarians in Long Island high schools alike—is just about the most powerful idea in yettie culture. Out here, dude, you can do *anything*.

No group of yetties believes in this rugged frontiersman's dream more seriously (nor more naively) than the Mouse Jockeys. Mouse Jockeys are those reasonably bright young men and women raised on computers and MTV, who are now stifling their self-styled creativity in the name of cube-farming temp work for a large corporate entity that allows them to dress in whatever manner they choose and to take free low-fat, no-foam triple lattes at the dispensaries installed on every floor of their office. To the Mouse Jockey this sort of existence still calls up images of a border town, one crowded with visions of the *Star Wars* bar scene, sex with women who look like *Tomb Raider*'s Lara Croft, the possibility of great wealth and near-heroic acts. Mouse Jockeys believe in that dream. They almost have to, despite—or perhaps because of—the paradox of their lowly place in the New Economy. Dreams make a 90-hour workweek more palatable.

Mouse Jockeys ride comfortable chairs in front of glowing monitors in anonymous cubicles that stretch out across gigantic office spaces in old lofts in San Francisco's Soma district, or high above lower Broadway or the Hudson River in Manhattan. They work their mice over developing Web sites in L.A. and Austin and Chicago and Boston, and they code copy and drop in images for e-commerce ventures in Dallas and Kansas City. They write. They scan. They stack Zip disks like cordwood and complain about lack of space on the server. Occasionally, they help develop software. But they're all jobbers, strictly work-for-hire, and high-level Codewriting Geeks scoff at them for it: "Clothes by Gap, coding by skills gap," one e-mailed me in response to a question about Mouse Jockey culture. "These people are to software development what *Beverly Hills 90210* is to *Citizen Kane.*"

Mouse Jockeys are the educated working class of the New Economy. A Mouse Jockey might be a Content Provider, for instance, writing "editorial" for Web sites both commercial and literary. Or he might be a novelist moonlighting as a Web-site coding man-about-town, otherwise known as a Geek Literatus. He might be a Professional Beta Tester, or a low-level Web designer of the Designer Girl persuasion. Mouse Jockeys, as upper-class Britons used to say of black-smiths who read Edmund Burke, may have *notions*. Mouse Jockeys might believe, for instance, that their jobs are just stepping-stones to the untold riches provided those who risk capital in the name of new things, big ideas, art. But they're in their mid-20s and fall into distinct types all the same.

The Content Provider

SO IT'S LIKE this. You're in high school, and you hang out on this really shaky bridge you built between the nerd world over in the computer-science lab and the more popular one that throws parties all the time and gets good grades and better pot.

You're a girl. You're pretty good friends with some varsity boys. Also with some of the trenchcoated weirdos you know not to be weirdos at all, but really kind of sweet. You've known that crowd of misfits since forever. One of them lives next door. Your girlfriends run to the same mix as the boys: Cindy the Science Geek and Amy the Actress vie in your attentions for best-pal status. You've known them since second and fourth grade, respectively. They don't even know one another.

You edit the school paper and stage-manage the school's production of *Picnic*. You bid liberal arts for college and end up amid ivy and Birkenstocks somewhere in New England, beneath wide hills that don't quite pass for mountains, where you discover poetry. Also that the geeks and weirdos, with the help they gave you with the computer your dad brought home in seventh grade, with the awkward, friendly, kiss-your-brother conversations you had with them all through high school, with their strange, muted presence in your life, have truly taught you well. You have a T1 line into your dorm room and find that you *get* the principles by which the Internet works and that you understand the power of the Web as a delivery system for information. You understand the architecture, can even write a little HTML. You debug the college literary magazine's Web site and land an editor's slot. And continue to write poems.

Graduate. Move to New York on the promise of a gig reading manuscripts for George Plimpton at the *Paris Review* and $11 an hour doing research for the guy who taught creative nonfiction your senior year. You've read his stories in *The New Yorker*. It's a good start.

And it is, until the parties at Plimpton's house begin to wear you down, and the research dries up, and Cindy calls out of the blue from San Francisco to say she's creating Web sites for brick-and-mortar retail outfits and just bought a two-bedroom house in the Mission. It all falls to pieces then. You haven't written a poem in 16 months. You're maxed out on your Visa. You have three roommates in a two-bedroom apartment on East 87th Street. Cindy bought a *house*?

"Really?" you say. And just like that, you end up a Content Provider. You write blurbs for Cindy at first: dozens and dozens

① **Cat-eye glasses frames**, with rhinestones she glued on one night for a party. Sometimes she finds herself whimsical like that.

② **Antique cardigan** sweater, purchased at a small clothing store in Williamsburg, Brooklyn, for about what it would have cost new in 1961. With the Boy George T-shirt, it finishes the apotheosis of Mouse Jockey sweater-set fashion. The Content Provider's older brother was really, really into Boy George at the time that Boy George was a non-ironic hipster icon. By buying the shirt, she honored her family.

③ **Messenger bag** containing an iBook (in tangerine), a copy of the fifth issue of the comic literary journal *McSweeney's*, fresh from its print-ing in Iceland, a sheaf of paper scrawled with notes toward a Web site selling fruit baskets for friends, family, and business associates, a half-eaten bag of Peanut M&Ms, 78 cents, two expired Metrocards for the subway, a hairbrush, today's *New York Times*, five card-stock flyers for friends' bands, art exhibits, and performances, and three Bic pens.

④ The Content Provider writes the Web site copy for these cool **rubber face plates for mobile phones**; she walked from the gig with a phone for herself and the whole spectrum of rubber gloves for it. Now, monthly, she's a 1000-minute girl.

⑤ Internet time moves at a far faster rate than real time. Thus the Content Provider feels that her **Razor scooter** is actually a retro move—recall-ing those distant days in early 2000 when only five-year-olds had them.

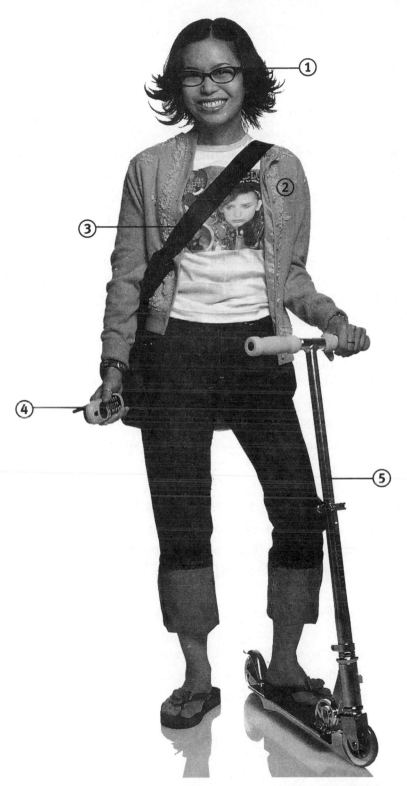

of 43-word treatises on pressure-treated lumber, Makita planers, Kohler faucets. This is "content" for a Web site: Doityourselfer.com or something. You don't even know. Cindy puts these things up on the Web next to pictures of the products, and armchair carpenters in Topeka click on the icon and buy. You do this for a candy-company site, for a business-to-business franchise, for some guy selling wine. You learn a lot about Sauvignon grapes. At the New York launch of the wine site, you see a nerd from college, who asks shyly what you're doing. You say, and he smiles. He needs writers himself, he says, suddenly not shy at all. Something about streaming video comes out of his mouth, and then about news, poetry, art. He's CEO of what-ever it is. He's made good.

So three weeks later you've got a cubicle on lower Broadway and the mandate to write 200-word reviews of, like, art. Once, twice a day, five days a week: The company needs content that will draw traffic to its site. Hits. Be controversial, says the CEO, the Nerd Made Good. There's an office party every Friday, with margaritas. You make $60,000 a year, and your package started with 5,000 stock options. It'll go up next year if you stick around to vest. Amy's waiting tables in West Hollywood and just had her breasts done. You call her some-times from the cubicle. She doesn't have e-mail. You get a trib-al tattoo on your ankle. Guys begin to talk to you at parties in ways they haven't before. Self-confidence blooms in you like a rose.

Content Providers still live on high school's precarious bridge. They're often caught between the Geekocile and the in-crowd. They wear fashionable eyeglasses that reflect this position: chic yet nerdy, hopefully radiating *intelligence*. Their clothes are Banana Republican tricked down with thrift-store sweaters, cocktail dresses on the weekends. If male, the gear runs gray and black for meetings with bosses, and skaterin-Geranimals for sitting around the apartment writing e-commerce haiku. Occasionally Actual Modern Fiction ensues, and friends put it on other Web sites or in zines made up to be magazines. They get smiles at the bar on Saturday night, and occasional dates.

The Content Provider is only writing for the Web for now. She's got a few book ideas. And her poetry. But she tells no one about this, because there is actually a part of her that understands the medium to be the single greatest boon to writing since Gutenberg's press. That people won't read long pieces on screen, she feels, is a fact sure to change. Some bright young thing will come up with better technology and we will all, suddenly, read everything over a monitor of some kind. We will. Won't we?

If not, she figures, there's always graduate school.

The Geek Literatus

The Geek Literatus hacks code for Web sites. Freelance. College gave him a degree in medieval literature and four years of 30-hour weeks on his computer. The Geek Literatus writes science fiction when he isn't working for an Internet company, or sometimes when he is, and ships the stories off to magazines and Web sites hoping to get published. Once he wrote a spec script for *Deep Space Nine*. It's up on the Web somewhere. He took it off his own Web site three days after losing his virginity to a "womyn" he met at a Society for Creative Anachronism meeting. That was years ago. The script was kind of lame, and he was embarrassed about it.

The Geek Literatus reads a lot of novels. He has seen a great number of films, more in fact than anyone he has ever met on the customer side of a video-store front desk. He likes TV. His first magazine subscription was to *Discover*. His latest was to

(1) Triple-shot whole milk grande *latte* with wings. It's his fourth of the day.

(2) *Coke-bottle lenses*. Born nearsighted, the Geek Literatus spent a lot of time in very dimly-lit rooms as a child, making his bad eyesight worse. Spending twelve hour days in front of a glowing Mac monitor doesn't help matters. But the Malcolm X frames do much to compensate. They profile *hip*.

(3) *Black-ink pen*. See, the guy has a *journal*, where he keeps ideas for the novel and impressions of people he sees on the subway. He's not just a cube-living HTML coder after all; he has an intellectual, writerly lifestyle.

(4) New model *Danish school bag*, an update on the version his third-grade teacher in the gifted-and-talented program had. He's got his phone clipped to the front (programmed to speed dial his mom, the burrito place, and the art cinema downtown), and lapel buttons for Charles Manson and Black Flag. The former's a punk signifier; the latter simple homage to a time when Henry Rollins wasn't an asshole. Within the bag: a copy of *Red Herring* (there's an article about a site he worked on in this month's issue), some printouts from Inside.com relating to same, a copy of Neal Stephenson's *In the Beginning…Was the Command Line*, two Pavement CDs, a sale's receipt for a first edition of *The Illuminatus Trilogy*, which was a wedding gift for his best friend from grade school, his coffee-stained journal notebook, and a Panasonic portable CD player with Koss headphones.

(5) *Black khakis*, from Banana Republic. In wallet: driver license, Visa card, Mookie Wilson baseball card from his last year with the Mets, video-rental card, $60 in cash because he's going out to hear a band tonight, burrito receipts for his notional dinner-expense account, Sensor card for getting into the offices late at night, and a small sheet of paper on which he's written some neat words: gloaming; tetrad; sanguine.

(6) *Steve Madden shoes*, which are to Geek Literati as white rubber boots are to Louisiana shrimp fishermen.

eCompany Now. He reads *The New York Review of Books* as well, because he's heard that the staff there uses only type-writers and this amuses him, as do the letters the magazine prints. He doesn't sleep much. He got an 800 on the math portion of the SAT and told no one. His thing in high school was English. He scored a 4 on the Advanced Placement litera-ture exam and almost wept. He told no one about that either.

The Geek Literatus works six months a year. More accu-rately, he works six months a year for *money.* Six months a year he works on his novel, which concerns the story of a young Druid teleported into suburban Detroit circa 2013, where he meets and falls in love with a kindergarten teacher who used to be a cryptographer at the National Security Admin-istration. They fight evil together and sometimes teleport into historical events as they actually happen. It's cool. More litera-ture than sci-fi. He sends chapters out to friends, and they offer comments. He hasn't found a publisher yet.

The rest of the time, the Geek Literatus writes HTML. HTML is a simple computer language that tells the Web browser on your computer, as data comes flying in over your phone line from the home page of Funnypandas.com or wherever, how the text and graphics should be displayed on your screen. It does so via something called HTTP, which is the HyperText Transfer Protocol. HTTP is an agreement that defines a univer-sal method of transmitting data, so that the funny panda on your Mac goes in the same place as on any other computer screen in the world. No matter what machine you use, the funny panda is the same—and thanks to another computer language the Geek Literatus knows passingly well, Java, it does the same funny dance on whatever computer system calls it up. That's what Geek Literati do: make sure the panda materializes on your screen, that he dances, and that you can click on him to make a purchase or jump to another area of the site.

HTML is basically, as the novelist Neal Stephenson has written, a telegram; it provides terse descriptions of events that your Web browser, like a baseball announcer reading telegraph copy in the early days of radio, uses to create the whole and complete picture of events: *Ty Cobb at the plate. A whistling fastball and* crack, *Cobb mashes a tater!* Before the announcer read it aloud, that sentence was simple code—a lifeless series of dots and dashes. It can be grueling work, coding those dashes and dots. But the Geek Literatus enjoys it. He likes courting burnout on freelance jobs that last for months. He likes the social aspect of the race to finish a product—the eating of late-night pizzas and the getting of cans of orange soda from the fridge near the elevators and the blushing frisson he feels when that girl who writes content drops by to ask a question about how she can code her own copy. And he likes the work itself. Coding for Web sites requires the sort of thinking the Geek Literatus does best—impersonal and exact thinking, to be precise about it—and when someone from management drops by his cubicle to commend him on a repaired link or replaced tag of some sort, it can set the Geek Literatus to buzzing. It sets him to buzzing because he's pleased to have done something obvious and smart, pleased to have been, for a moment, *studly.* Plus, he gets to hang out with the Designer Girl sometimes, and the Designer Girl is, as he doesn't mind e-mailing his friends from college (who usually treasure his letters for their verbal acuity), *hot.*

The Geek Literatus wears khakis and a tucked-in dark button-down over a T-shirt that reads TAKE BACK THE NIGHT. He got it at a rally in Berkeley a while ago, trying to impress a woman he was trying to date. It didn't work. He has square-tipped black lace-ups from Kenneth Cole for work and hightop Converse All Stars for home. He lives in a clean and carpeted apartment, with a computer system that is about 10 times more powerful than he needs to write science fiction and posts for computer bulletin boards devoted to arcane subjects he's not even sure he cares about anymore. He owns a lot of books. His TV is small. He's had the same stereo since high school and still owns a fair amount of vinyl. The Geek Literatus listens to metal when he's vacuuming his carpet. He sets the radio to NPR when he's making dinner, and pets his cat as he eats.

The Designer Girl

THE THING about the Designer Girl is, she doesn't really design. She thinks *about* design, and also about Foucault, and the latest issue of *nest*, and about last night at a bar in the Mission and the blue cowboy hat she wore. She thinks about these things and draws big, inspirational pictures on the whiteboards in the conference room with the buffed faux rustic table in it. She checks her messages on her mobile phone—she doesn't even *have* a land-line office phone—and she checks her stocks on Ameritrade every time she checks her e-mail, which is pretty much constantly since it chirps nicely at her when mail arrives in her in-box. She goes to a lot of meetings and talks grandiloquently about "organic value" and "multimedia cross-platforming." The Designer Girl does all this, and she goes out at lunch to sit on the grass in South Park, in San Francisco, and she eats dolphin-free tuna salad niçoise from Café Centro. She goes there in the mornings, too, though just for morning meetings, not for food. She doesn't, like, hang out in South Park or anything.

The Designer Girl is 24. She works at a Web-design firm in Soma that bids on companies that need "hip" and "edgy" the way Wal-Mart needs serious acreage just outside small cities that don't have a Kmart or a Sears. The Designer Girl *is* hip and edgy. She says so, all the time, in a semi-ironic tone of voice she perfected in 11th grade. It's her own personal marketing tool.

The Designer Girl wears wire-frame glasses with yellow lenses. They look like something Lindsay Wagner wore on *The Bionic Woman*. She wears tops that reveal her flat stomach and small, gold belly-button ring. Her daily uniform also includes Helmut Lang pants and slides that are too expensive for her salary, which is low but comes with stock options should her firm go public. Which it might, you know. Not that she got into this to be rich. She has shoulder-length hair that can look mussed and playful and arty. For meetings with clients, she can spray it into a virtual helmet.

The Designer Girl was into the visual arts in college. Also comparative literature. And critical theory. She's lurked around left-leaning listservs devoted to subverting the cultural hegemony of the Web, and she believes deeply in the notion that an artist's goal in this new century should be to synthesize the newly unformattable world. She digs the old-media artist Jeff Koons, who started calling his work a form of artificial intelligence. It is! All art is. She has two tattoos. One's on her back, peeking up from the top of her thong, a sort of Gaelic design she saw in a show catalog from the Whitney a few years ago, which reminded her of her grandfather. The other's a green star. It's on her ankle. She touches it sometimes, for luck.

The Designer Girl has a boyfriend. He was in a band for a while; they set Edward Gorey lyrics to bubblegum pop and played out for a year or two as the Deaf Mexicans. Now he's a DJ, playing retro grunge and really-obscure-in-the-U.S. jungle beats. He works in the telephony industry. In sales. He's the guy the suits bring along to show that the company has street credibility and youth at its core, that it's going places, fast. He gave her the newest MP3 player for her birthday a month ago, programmed with the new Prince Paul and a lot of ambient

1. ***Bionic Woman glasses***, with smoked yellow lenses, intimating both intelligence and style.

2. ***Gold chain***, for that Italian dirty-girl feel. It works best in meetings, and at the bar.

3. ***Air-brushed T-shirt***, which is post-post-post ironic enough to rate as high fashion among the *Wired* set.

4. ***Mobile phone***, for calling into the office from South Park lunches. American Spirit cigarette, because she's trying to quit and thought, because of the lame kerning of the letters, that the "non-additive tobacco" disclaimer on the box read "non-addictive tobacco." Oh, well.

5. ***Helmut Lang pants***. She has three pair, purchased by a friend in New York who works in the art department at *Marie Claire*.

6. ***Yak Pak*** quasi-messenger bag, containing: a subscription copy of *Silicon Alley Reporter* (she wants to move to New York), stick concealer, lip gloss, three OB tampons, two Zip disks with work projects on them, a new copy of *Flash Web Design*, a Palm V, a diaphragm, three packs of matches from the W Hotel, a tank top and shorts for yoga class, and a Mexican change purse with her California driver's license in it, along with a Visa card, $41, three ounces of change, and the keys to her apartment and bike lock.

7. On her ankle, under the pants, a ***tattoo*** of a Pantone Color Chip, with its accompanying number: 466C. Her skin tone!

8. ***Way-high heels***, which the Designer Girl wears only on the first and last days of freelance jobs, to create an impression. The rest of the time it's retro "trainers" of the English rave-kid model.

9. ***iMac***. Apple is her afro, her dashiki, her culture, her life.

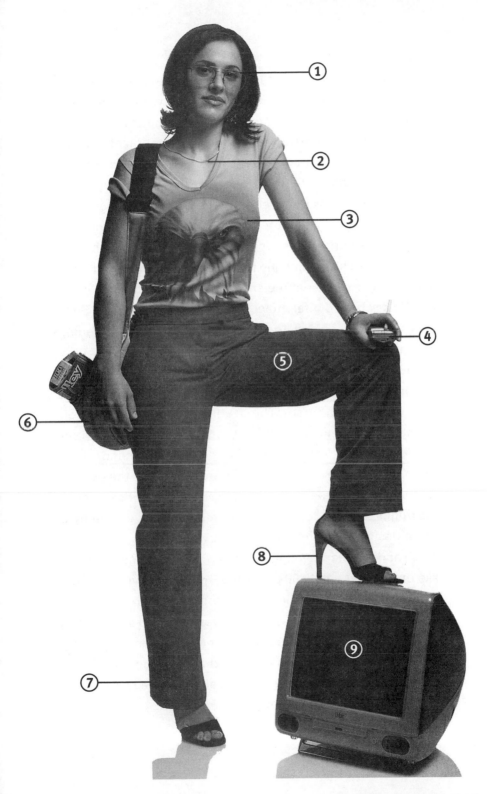

dub. He's awesome. Sometimes, at his house on a dewy Sunday morning, she'll draw him sleeping, with a nice pen she bought for that task, on the back of a phone bill or something. He tacks the portraits up on his workstation at the office.

They don't sleep much at her place. The Designer Girl has a lot of roommates. They all crowd into this much-too-small house near the Rock Ridge stop on BART and try to have dinner together, or leave for the night together, at least once a week. The Designer Girl's room has a Macintosh G4 in it, which she convinced her father she needed for freelance work, and on it she does do some freelance design, and surfs the Web, and thinks about digital movies she'd like to be editing. She does some print design, too, for friends with gallery openings or CD releases. She calls herself a Queen of Quark.

The Designer Girl likes her daily schedule. She comes in around 9:30 and reads her e-mail, checking to see if there are any "emergencies" afoot. The deadlines on her current projects are a long time off, so there probably won't be. Then she surfs the Web until 10:15, when her project team heads out to South Park to meet. The managers are there, and the geeky site builders and freelance coders and the senior designers. She might get a job for the afternoon out of that, executing a senior designer's whim. Then it's back to the office for more e-mail and another meeting before lunch. Meetings and e-mail take up approximately 60 percent of her time. Give a few 15-minute slots of the afternoon to flirty behavior on the smoking deck in the back of the loft, and the Designer Girl spends only 20 percent of her time actually working on a client's design.

Which is the only part of the day that bums her out. The clients are *so* pedestrian. They're all about strategy. She's thinking about going freelance full-time soon.

The Professional Beta Tester

THE PROCESS BY which a piece of software makes its way from the programmer's mighty brain to the soft, sweaty hands of the consumer at the local computer store is a fairly simple one, so long as you ignore the difficulty of actually writing the thing. The programmer writes his program. And then the programmer's minions test the hell out of it, aiming to reveal and repair its bugs in order to make it work correctly on every computer that could conceivably ever download and use it.

There are generally two phases of this product testing. The first is the "alpha test," in which the software is tested for functionality and stability. The second is the "beta test," in which the product is used in controlled situations that are meant to mimic real-world applications. Beta testers use the software. They log the bugs they find on it and offer feedback on the program to the programmer. They hope in turn to receive his high regard for their comments.

Beta testing is itself divided into two kinds of product examination. There is the public kind, in which sad-eyed teenage volunteer boys in Skokie bedrooms run buggy new role-playing games into the night, so that they may be the first in their ward to have reached level seven in *Ankh: The Questing* and take part in the thing's eventual "perfection." They are baby yetties, these amateurs, and I won't trouble you with them here. Secondarily, though, there is a private kind of beta testing, run by and for the company, with its team of in-house Professional Beta Testers. And these animals deserve our attention.

The Professional Beta Tester longs to be a programmer. He was born and remains an only, lonely child, who excelled as a youth in mathematics and spatial arrangements and raced through both Algebra I and II by the middle of sixth grade. At that time his parents purchased a small PC, which he appropriated for himself immediately and had upgraded to an XT by the time he was in junior high school. His next computer was a

① Respectable *spectacles* for the geek in your life. Worn not with pride but with absolute indifference.

② *Mobile phone* on the shoulder strap, company-issued. Numbers programmed into it reach his product manager, his former roommate who now works at Oracle and with whom he's trying to develop a business plan, his *other* product manager, and the two other testers on his team.

③ *Backpack* for Frisbee and clothes for low-key Ultimate game later this afternoon—a Kozmo.com T-shirt and cut-off khaki shorts. Also: a plastic baggie with a half-ounce of middling grade marijuana, a pipe shaped like a hobbit, and a new mouse to replace the one on his home-built super machine at the apartment, which wore out after too many games of Quake.

④ Grande *chai latte*. Don't tell anyone. He likes the sweet of it, to tell the truth. Better than Jolt.

⑤ *Skytel pager*. Why? He's virtually *always* in his cube, 18 inches from his phone. Those damn product managers again! Always with the leash!

⑥ *Sports watch*, waterproof so that he doesn't lose another one to the shower, where he always forgets to remove it.

⑦ **Fletch Won**, by Gregory McDonald. The Professional Beta Tester spends a lot of time reading comic books, but is happy to take time out once in a while to read McDonald, whose hipster-geek detective was first played on the screen by Chevy Chase, who is kind of a cool guy if you think about it logically.

⑧ *Untied shoelace*. Sign of a Professional Beta Tester out of the mating season.

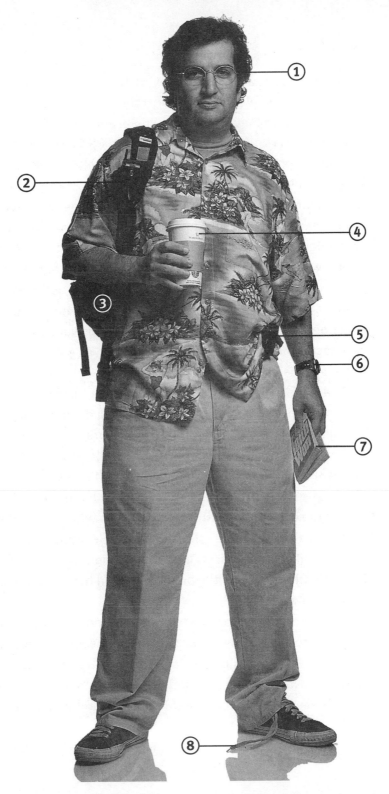

Northgate 386DX20, which he loved; he keeps the original keyboard on a shelf above his workstation at home. He built a 486DX2/66 after that, and then a P5-90, and a P5-166. The machine in his bedroom office today is a P5-200MMX. It's *fast*.

The Professional Beta Tester is largely self-educated. His massive suburban high school *sucked*, in his humble opinion, and the three years he spent at the state college were even worse, except for the computer labs. He has taught himself computer languages: BASIC, Pascal, C, and most recently C++. He knows UNIX from college. He believes in the notion of a technocracy, though he does not articulate this belief. He longs to be a part of a technocracy. That's why he dropped out of school to take a job with a pretty huge software company, beta testing. Yes! They take in $200 million a year at this place. Thanks to his hard work.

The Professional Beta Tester sits in his cubicle on the company's campus and rarely leaves. When he does, he repairs to a small, lightless apartment that houses, principally, his home computer. Also a stunning number of comic books and technical manuals. There's a ballcap he got at the first COMDEX convention he ever attended, three years ago, hanging on the outside of the door to the bathroom. He notes with some pride that he has *never* cleaned the bathroom. He enjoys a pork burrito over all other foods. He kind of digs the Dave Matthews Band. Matthews has a little bit of a belly on him. He seems like a fellow traveler.

The Professional Beta Tester will be an entrepreneur soon. He wants to be. Access to his company's resources, and the awesome amount of time he has spent testing its products and speaking with its managers and programmers and with his peers, have given him an idea of the sort that he thinks might qualify as big, the sort of product that in five years' time everyone will think of as water. Everyone will use it. That's the sort of thing you want: simple and indispensable. The market cap for that is impossible for the Professional Beta Tester to imagine. He could be bigger than France.

The Professional Beta Tester has given NDAs to his parents on this idea, and to two friends, one from the company and one from college. They'll be his CIO and COO, respectively. They're all reading business books, all the time. And the Professional Beta Tester has been scanning *The Industry Standard* weekly for trends, waiting on his moment. His friend from college knows someone who knows someone at Draper, Fisher, Jurvetson. They'll gin up a business plan in the next month or so, then get it out there to the VC. There's always money for ideas like water. The market will love it.

In the meantime, the Professional Beta Tester has 70 hours of work to complete by Friday. The dream keeps him awake and alert: He will be a Mouse Jockey no more!

FINALLY, THE PILOTFISH: E-ARTISTES, MARKET ANALYSTS, AND JOURNALISTS

AND SO THE hydra-headed yettie leviathan makes its way through oceans of capital and seas of profit and loss, into the uncharted, storm-tossed waters off Cape Future. We've met CEOs and Programmers thus far, VCs and Barristers, Crossover Geezers, Salesbots, PR Bunnies, Biz-Devs, Marketing Geeks, and Mouse Jockeys both high and low. But not yet the Pilotfish who swim beneath the whale, riding currents of love and hate, then feeding off the New Economy's scraps in great gnashing orgies of jealousy, rapture, contempt, and joy.

Antipathy! A tincture of scorn in the happy ocean! Pilotfish are e-artiste technocrats, eager to reflect in soft screen light the deep and sober reality of all the Internet provides and will provide. Pilotfish are market analysts, who pick and choose tech-sector stocks from afar, deciding which e-entity is up and which is down, or headed down, or potentially up; they grade the yettie world and pray that those who see their grades will heed them, else their words will not move markets, and they will waste away. And pilotfish are journalists who write about the Web, who grudgingly report the rise and gleefully chronicle the fall of dot.com fortunes, who weave and unweave all the intricacies of the New Economy and that which it portends. Beneath the broad and bloated stomach of the giant yettie beast, the Pilotfish declare themselves shaded and safe—in other words, cool.

The E-Artiste

THE E-ARTISTE is wearing some sort of postapocalyptic clown shoes on her feet, and she's standing there in the foyer of this bistro down on the Williamsburg side of the East River in New York, with her mousy hair pulled into tight ponytails, two of them out of the sides of her head, like flying buttresses keeping her brain in place, and she's saying that the computer—the computer as an object, no matter which computer it is—is just a more highly evolved version of the Etch A Sketch she had as a child. The computer is familiar like that. It's familiar to all of us, she says. It's something we've always known and therefore trusted. As a child, we knew: You twiddle the dials and out comes the picture. As grownups, we know: You slide the mouse around and out comes the picture. An Etch A Sketch, no more than that.

The E-Artiste came up with this idea one day after riding her bicycle across the Williamsburg Bridge to a temp job at an advertising shop on Broadway just below Houston: ads for startup businesses, all the time. The place was really cool and weird, she thought, with its European-by-way-of-San-Francisco-and-Manhattan aesthetic and a staff that ran to former rock guitarists, Cooper Union grads, a few hipster Syracuse dudes, and a smattering of film-school geeks on the serious make. They all worked in a big, spare, open space, with G4's and video monitors everywhere and a support staff that wasn't so much ethnically diverse as ethnically intoxicated; the receptionist up front by the elevator was Anglo-Cherokee on her mother's side and Tutsi-Vietnamese on her father's. The E-Artiste worked there as a freelance Mouse Jockey for six weeks, helping one of the Syracuse dudes on an e-business campaign, doing graphic design.

The place was cool, she told her friends, but the job itself was lame. Corny even. She didn't like the designs they wanted

1. ***Sony digital camera***. A gift from her father. Well, sort of. The E-Artiste charged it on the Visa he gave her for "emergencies" and explained it to him as a rent-barter deal that she had to commit to or else *lose her apartment*. He took the hook, and now the E-Artiste uses the camera to document her life.

2. ***Librarian's glasses***, also purchased on Dad's credit card, last summer when she went south to visit the family. She'd been wearing old Ray-Ban Wayfarers then, with clear prescription lenses, and her mother almost fainted when she saw her daughter in them. "Why, you look like a bug!" Mom had said, and looked to cry.

3. ***Twin ponytails***. One on each side of the head, pulled tight and childlike to create the impression and feeling of innocence so important to the creation of art.

4. ***Motorola mobile phone***. The E-Artiste doesn't speak too frequently about how she can afford to keep this service up along with her two home lines, but friends are too polite to ask.

5. ***Mom's cardigan***, brought up to New York after last Christmas, when the E-Artiste fished the thing out of a bag destined for the thrift shop at the local Baptist church. She wears it over a tank top ever-so-slightly stained at the underarms.

6. ***Backpack***. It's one of those plastic-body numbers that looks like the motor casing for a particularly powerful home vacuum cleaner, and it cost her the better part of two days' pay. But she can keep her iBook in there without it getting banged around too badly, along with all that she needs to stay in Manhattan for a full day of work and play: water, aspirin, sketchbook, lip balm, sunscreen, extra underwear, and a nylon wallet with $3 and that helpful Visa card.

7. The skirt's ***faux Burberry*** anti-fashion, and combines with the pony-tails and the top gear to give the E-Artiste the feeling that she's wickedly professional, amusingly subversive: The outfit's her going-to-the-city temp wear.

8. Post-apocalyptic ***clown shoes***, from a company called Whoosh. Your E-Artiste in a nutshell.

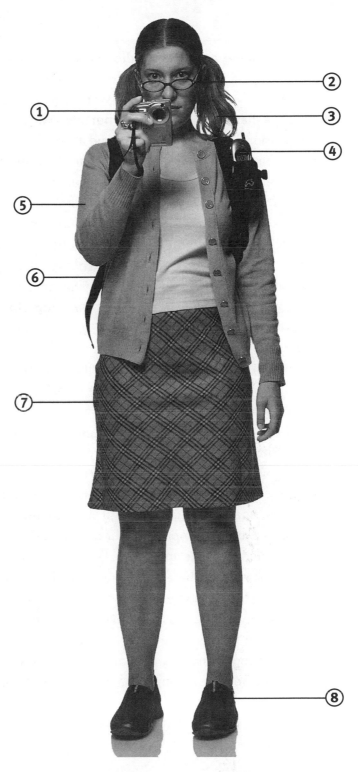

her to emulate, and she sure didn't like the way this one particular Syracuse dude kept hitting on her—telling her how clean
her layouts were, asking did she want to go grab a beer later,
crap like that. She didn't know what to do with that. She needed the money, was all she knew, and an Idea. The Idea, she felt,
would get her some funding, a place to show the art the Idea
would engender. It would give her an actual *place* in the city
she's lived in anonymously for four years. The E-Artiste was 26
when she thought all this. She longed for fame.

And then one afternoon a shaft of light came streaming in
from the windows on the south side of the building, and it
played off her monitor in such a way that she thought, really
suddenly, *This is an Etch A Sketch. This program I'm
working*—Quark, as it happened—*is just a higher-tech version
of an Etch A Sketch*. The E-Artiste quit the job that afternoon,
bought an original Etch A Sketch at the Toys "Я" Us in Union
Square, and spent the next five days messing around with it at
home.

The E-Artiste actually has a background in computer science. She was the scary-smart weird chick in her high school
class down in Charleston, South Carolina, and hit the 99th per-
centile on every math or science achievement test they threw
at her. Her hair was blue then, and she was into straight-edge
hardcore and the computer in her banker dad's den. The boys
in their madras shirts and Duck's Head chinos wouldn't talk to
her for money. She hated that, and hated herself for hating it.
They were awful people.

College, though, she loved. Went to the University of the
South up in Tennessee and did a tremendous amount of just-
for-kicks programming on top of her course load. Also: met
some nice boys, saw some great rock shows, began to make
art. New York City sang for her as the Sirens did for Odysseus.
Until a year ago, she was freelance design, freelance Web

coding, freelance *anything*. She lived over in Williamsburg, argued with art geeks on anarchist listservs from the back of the loft she shared with two jugglers, a brick sculptor, and three dogs, and simply got by. The Etch-a-Sketch day changed all that.

The E-Artiste has a gallery show coming up, in a raw space on West 30th Street, way west. It's her third in 18 months. She has all these antiquated monitors she scored from a Mouse Jockey friend who runs the IT department at a private bank downtown, and she's hooked them up to some really, really obsolete old Macs, and using these and some sporty, old-school programming, she's done some childlike drawings, dusty slate lines over a light-gray monitor background. They sell like crazy, these things! E-art! She has a Web site, a new PalmPilot, and a German boyfriend who was a chemical engineer and now sells vintage stereo equipment out of a storefront in Tribeca. The loft in Williamsburg's all theirs now; she hasn't seen her old roommates in about a year. She and Dieter are thinking about buying a place up in Hudson, for weekends, and for making art. But first the E-Artiste has a couple of interviews to do, and then a meeting with some clients from Palo Alto, and then dinner with some people from her gallery. Her secret truth? She couldn't draw a stick-figure family if you spotted her the heads and the arms.

"Golly, art's just binary code," she says, shaking her pony-tails. "It's a product just like software. Only prettier."

The Analyst

THE ANALYST likes to tell you how it is. And how it will be, because of how it was. She's about the Information. She's 29 years old, an economics major out of Penn State with six years' experience on Wall Street calling tech stocks *out*. She's

(1) **Double-breasted pantsuit** that might have belonged to the Analyst's aunt, who worked on Wall Street in the mid-1980s. It didn't; the Analyst bought the thing new when she got her latest job.

(2) **IBM laptop**, firm-issued. The Analyst works the Information on this machine, playing with spreadsheets like that guy in Phish with his guitar, working the numbers back and forth.

(3) **Heels over knee-his**. The Analyst is among the last young women in America to wear hose regularly to work, and one of only a few of these not to complain about it. She *likes* hose, actually, likes the feel of it coming off her ankles after a long day, and the way it slides on the rough fabric of her office carpet when she's sitting in her Aeron like Kirk on the bridge of the *Enterprise*.

(4) **L.L. Bean "boat tote,"** her third since college. A boyfriend gave it to her on the occasion of their trip to Maine to visit his grandparents. The relationship went Chapter 11 two weeks later, but the bag's still the bee's knees. In it: today's *Wall Street Journal*, which she reads in the black car that takes her to work every morning at 5:45 A.M.; a towel and gym clothes for the workout she will, once again, blow off in favor of getting more work done; a Panasonic portable CD player with Hole's *Live Through This* in it—Courtney Love's voice, to the Analyst, is a battle cry, and when she sings "I want to be the girl with the most cake," the Analyst feels a chill of understanding; a bottle of Fiji water; and her mobile phone.

(5) **Slingbag by Coach**, in which the Analyst keeps the keys to her apartment, her wallet (four credit cards, a corporate Amex, driver's license, company ID, passport, $35, and a fat packet of dinner receipts [Nobu, Next Door Nobu, Tomoe Sushi, Sushisay, Blue Ribbon Sushi, Nobu again]). Also a half-used book of matches from the Fairmont Hotel in San Jose and a full pack of Marlboro Lights. Lip gloss. Two business cards from would-be suitors. One guy's a publishing lackey; the other a bond trader at a big, big firm. She'll call neither one of them. She's about work right now, and the future.

been New Economy bullish from way back—a high-tech original gangster who has never been tempted to cross the Rubicon and mess around with a startup. No way. All those smelly little geeks with their risible little monitor pets and boxed *Matrix* dolls and unshowered pong? Please. The Analyst built her core model right here on Wall Street. And she likes it on Wall Street just fine, a smart girl amid the big, swinging dicks. My atavistic boys, she thinks of them, clench-necked and ever-so-slightly out of the loop with their shined cap-toes and off-the-rack suits. My brothers, she thinks of them.

The Analyst loves sushi—*loves* it. Sushi is in fact the only protein she eats, twice a day—once at her desk at lunch and the next time late and out in Soho, Noho, Nolita, someplace like that. Downtown Manhattan just like she pictured it as a little girl back home in Harrisburg, with futomaki everywhere, like batteries stacked at the Wal-Mart they built near her mom's. Then home to read annuals, quarterlies, red herrings, the business press, to consume more of the Information. The Analyst averages about four hours of sleep a night; she likes to be in the office early, to check on Japan. She drinks Diet Coke from the start of the day until her last one in bed and wears, 14 hours a day, the unfortunate pantsuit of a career-monster superwoman circa 1985. Armani awaits her, she feels. She'll buy when the forecast looks right.

The Analyst only smokes on weekends, and then only when she's drunk. Which isn't often, but when it is: Ketel martini, wet, three olives. She has a Samsung SCH 3500 mobile phone to keep in touch with her two real friends here in New York, both executives in the music industry and both, the Analyst feels, as doomed as ham-radio salesmen. She owns a Palm V, too, with a color screen, that she doesn't, in truth, use very much at all. Mostly she relies on her soft Coach slingbag, in which sits her microthin laptop, and always a fat few inches of paperwork to read. She is a member of the genius-kid organization Mensa and trumpeted the fact on her resumé. The senior analyst at her Wall Street firm, having hired her, told her to drop it—that it was a little gauche, a little weird. Well, she'd never! But the guy had rated AOL a buy back when AOL was using horses and wagons to get people their e-mail. He knew from the Information. She hit Delete on the Mensa line and has never mentioned it again.

The Analyst belongs to a gym near her apartment on Broome Street but hasn't gone in roughly three months. No time! She had a boyfriend in the final quarter of last year, a throwback jocko trading high-yield bonds for a firm full of dinosaurs. The sex came in way beneath expectations, though. And anyway: no time! The Analyst must read, scan, compute, make calls, read some more. Then *analyze,* in order to tell her clients just how it is that this e-commerce play or that one is a total lambada, as good as gone by the end of the month. It takes a strong stomach, she says, to play with tech stocks. They're bubbly. You never can tell. Well, *you* can't, she implies, twisting her high school signet ring on the pinky of her left hand. Not without the Information. "No growth here," she might say, into the phone clipped to her head at work like an airline reservationist's. "You want to hold." She'll never say "sell." She'll never say, "You don't want to catch a falling knife."

The Analyst lives to call, "Buy," and then watch as the stock soars and her brilliance gets reflected in its golden height. When that happens, it's deeply accretionary to her future earnings. She's an ambitious yettie, and she loves herself for that above all.

The Journalist

THERE IS A restaurant called Michael's on West 55th Street in Manhattan that serves as a sort of canteen for Old Economy media bigwigs. Michael's is an airy restaurant, with a Californian aesthetic that derives from the fact that the original Michael's is in Santa Monica, where it serves as a sort of canteen for Old Economy Hollywood bigwigs. The food at Michael's runs to good and oversize salads, simple fish dishes on the contempo-Californian model, roast chicken, mini-steaks; the drinking is limited to iced tea for those under 40 and white wine for those who are both older and eager to keep the spirit of the 1950s alive.

Michael's is about the last place on the planet you'd expect to hear something interesting or smart said about the New Economy. But one midday in the late spring of 2000 a question was asked there, by a ruddy-faced young corporate reporter of his Crossover Geezer mentor-cum-host, that may serve as an admirable introduction to the whole notion of the Pilotfish Journo: "So, how many stock options would I get?"

Welcome, crossover tyke! It is best to think of the Pilotfish Journalist as a kind of Content Provider Version 2.0, with analytical upgrades, less bothersome creativity, and a steeper learning curve. He doesn't provide mere content, like some comp-lit chucklehead writing faux e-erotica, but news. And what news it is. The Pilotfish Journalist covered crime for Wisconsin's *Burnt Toast Gazette* for a year after Yale, where the letter informing him that a *New Republic* internship would not be forthcoming had hit him with the force of a pillow soaked in joint compound; he had been the only *Yale Daily News* reporter in the class of '91 not to have gotten an interesting gig. He covered school boards after that, in New York at last, for a free weekly sheet that devoted more than a quarter of its editorial well to fawning portraits of local businesses that just happened to advertise opposite their praise. He picked up some stringer work on the side, reporting heard-on-the-street business news for a trade publication devoted to the glass industry, and parlayed the experience into a cub Internet business reporter's desk at a newsweekly hard up for talent. Where he flourished, if truth be known. Where he became a little star.

What could be more exciting, he had said to himself just the week before, cashing his paycheck for $632 after taxes, than to be first witness to the greatest creation of wealth in the history of the planet? To bring back to the People news of the progress of titans, of the slips and falls and reaches and grabs of Internet giants making their way across the Earth? To be the first to declare that Goaheaddoit.com actually can't, based on revenue projections leaked drunkenly in a bar? To be the first to know that it *can?* What access! What power!

But then again. The Pilotfish Journalist lives in a room—not a studio, but a room—on East 17th Street in Manhattan. He has a girlfriend he doesn't like much, a real estate rep for a large multinational firm, and $5,321.67 in Visa debt, left over from an ill-advised vacation he took at the end of last year with her and some chums from Yale, all of whom were involved in some way with the business end of the New Economy he himself covered. He loathes the poverty he feels, remembering that vacation, and remembering the debt, and thinking about his room on East 17th Street. *Is this it?* he wonders. *Is this all there is going to be?*

And so here he sits at this table at the center of the old-media world, in thrift-store gray tweed over loose black jeans, a pair of middle-management brogues on his feet, no tie, having lunch with his mentor. The Crossover Geezer across from him had left his place in the print world six months ago for a position as editorial director of an online business-to-business newsletter devoted to the highs and lows of the high-tech

① **Calvin Klein tie**, purchased at a discount shop for a friend's wedding in Westport, Connecticut, last summer. It is worn loose at the neck, in accordance with tabloid tough-guy style. Covering the yettie world, the Journalist is often the only person in the room wearing a tie; it is what marks him as a Pilotfish. When he moves to an online venture this year, he will lose it forever.

② Small, black, angular **glasses**. Imagine Buddy Holly as combined with Elvis Costello and accompanied by a dusting of pure geek and cold-pressed nerd. That's *it*!

③ **Extra pen**. When that chatty cathy Oracle flack starts talking, you can bet it's going to take a lot of ink.

④ **Notebook and microcassette combination**. In truth, the Journalist works almost exclusively from the recordings he makes. The notebook's only for "impressions" and e-mail addresses of potential sources. Also, potential song lyrics. The Journalist has a band.

⑤ **Swatch watch**. He'll go Tank when he gets to the Web, that's his feeling.

⑥ **Timbuk2 Messenger bag**. Contents: Compaq laptop computer, which has many gratifying nicks and scratches in its plastic casing (from reporting "on the road"), modem cables, spare computer battery, disks, file folders jammed with press releases and Nexis printouts, an issue of *Harper's*, pens, pencils, gum wrappers, paper clips, receipts from reporting trip to San Jose during which he was not allowed to stay at the Fairmont Hotel, goddamn it, and a matchbook with that girl from Jupiter Communication's e-mail written on it.

⑦ **Black jeans and Beatle boots**. Remember, he's in a *band*! In wallet: $20, bank card (checking balance $314), cancelled Visa card, business cards from last week's loft party, taxi receipts.

⑧ **Mobile phone**, mostly for show. His office won't pay for the airtime.

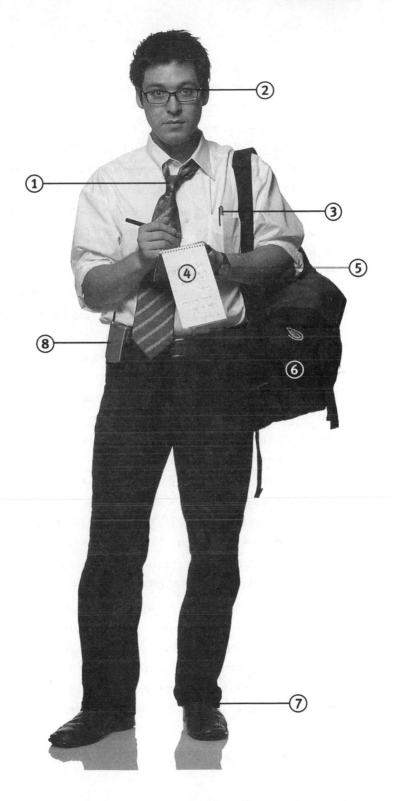

sphere. It's what they call a "sticky" site; readers are taking to it, coming back four, six, ten times a day. Investors, too. The company's primed to go public, maybe, once the market comes back strong for IPOs. Which it will! It must! The Crossover Geezer's taking our boy to lunch, offering him a position, a raise. The Pilotfish Journalist has $300 in his checking account and a Timex watch. He is primed and ready for more.

So, how many stock options would I get? To the Pilotfish Journalist, the New Economy is the best sort of game. Everyone gets to play. It's not like he's some rat pack sportswriter following millionaire skells around a locker room, on the road half the year listening to their crap for low money and incredible stress. It's not as if he has to parachute into war zones to watch conflicts escalate and little children die, and then attempt to explain that horror to people who aren't interested anyway, not when Cisco's about to release fourth-quarter earnings. It's not as if he's still covering crime, reporting out the tragic stupidity of people pushed just a little too far by circumstance, anger, fate. He is instead covering the single biggest story in the history of finance. The single biggest story in the history of the American culture. A story that is changing everything, even for him. He'll write for the Web, yes. So long as the Web gives back, as it has given back to so many.

The Pilotfish Journalist has small televisions at work and in his room, and a beater IBM clone he carries between the two. He generally files his reports on the markets from home. There's a poster of Che on his wall there, and a bookcase full of dog-eared used titles, most about newspapering, newspapermen, reportage. A blue glow from CNBC lights these up when he sits at his desk, using his bed as his chair, and writes. He has three phone lines. When he goes to the online place, he's getting DSL. Not for here, though. The Pilotfish Journalist is getting the fuck out of here.

8

CONCLUSION: YETTIES FOREVER

IT IS A CURIOUS thing to do when you're in the company of yetties, all of them with their angular little glasses so squarely aimed at the future, but let's look for a moment to the past. At the start of the *Field Guide*, I noted that the yuppie disappeared from the face of the planet sometime in late 1987, after that year's tumultuous stock-market crash. He disappeared just as the hippie had before him—the hippie starting to vanish as early as the dawn of the 1970s, as long hair moved from its place atop the heads of groovy college-kid antiwar protestors to beneath the hard hats of right-wing construction workers.

Still, the fundamental principles—the ethos—of both groups remained in cultural place, and moved along through the years, unto today. That is to say: The countercultural revolution of the 1960s was permanent, no matter how strenuously some hoary members of the Republican right deny it still. Those dirty, fornicating, long-haired and bell-bottomed hippies did their jobs, man: Because of them, the American populace, and the business interests it serves, became more open —forevermore!—to the notions of sex, drugs, rock 'n' roll, to class, gender, and race differences, even to spiritualism. Likewise, the Reagan revolution that begat the yuppie is ever-lasting, however screechingly those few aging members of the New Left dissent the facts. Greed is a given now, amigo. Big government sucks, dude. Deregulation is the shit. We are all, all of us, happy agents of capitalism—entrepreneurial souls one and all. A free-agent nation, to use the now ancient phrase, coined by *Fast Company* in 1997.

AND SO WE end where we began: over drinks at that self-same bar a short Razor scooter scoot from Silicon Alley, nearly 12 months after the first sighting of a yettie. They are all out tonight, in even more significant numbers than before. All of them—Content Providers, slick-rick Barristers, Mouse Jockeys, Geek Literati, a few Marketing Geeks and E-artistes, and, over in one of the corners nursing a rum and Coke, a Codewriting Geek in town for a few days to bring someone's peer-to-peer site up to where it can pre-launch. "It's like the next Napster," he says. "I can't say any more than that."

Peer-to-peer! One personal computer hooking up with another, exchanging bits, interacting, no middleman! P2P is the new B2B, which was for a while, ASP, or application service provider, which was the new e-commerce, which was the new push technology, which was something or other before that, unto the Early Days back in the early '90s, when everyone was still in high school. The technology changes in the New Economy occur so quickly that illustrating them can be a fool's game—before the image is even finished, it's time to begin again using a whole new series of variables, a whole new set of facts. It is, perpetually, time to refresh your browser.

And yet, as Po Bronson has asked rhetorically: Is the revolution over? So say the day-trading yettie bears, looking at a crazy-volatile market for tech stocks in the summer of 2000, looking at rising interest rates, at the end of IPO mania, at Amazon's dive. This Internet thing, this whole, strange high-tech racket, this yettie bazaar—it's over.

It isn't, of course. Not by a long shot. The yettie revolution is immutable. For good or for ill, it will never really go away.

And not just because this bar is packed with Banana Republicans, young women in cat-eye frames, Cibo Matto T-shirts, and expensive slacks, and baggy-panted skatepunks who have self-styled libertarian assistants back at the office to fetch them triple lattes. Yetties will survive not just because the maga-bibles of the New Economy have continued to grow despite April's market setbacks, some of them now capping the number of ads in each issue so that readers will not get lost amid all the clutter of a 400-page monthly. And they will thrive not simply because, as Nicholas Negroponte predicted in 1995, we are all becoming digital beings, each generation more so than the last. No, yetties will be a perpetual feature of the American landscape for only one simple reason: Yetties, capable of intelligent risk in the name of reward, and possessed of a high belief in the freedom that technology brings, have forever altered the way we look at the world around us, and the culture we develop within it.

Do not deny this, friends. Do not. We are all yuppies now, in some manner. We are all hippies now, too. And so, ineluctably, will we all soon become yetties—no matter what happens in the stock market, no matter how rigorously we avoid the charms of our digital future. Their culture, if not their software, will survive.

Think of that culture, then, as you step out tomorrow onto the sidewalks of yettievilles small and large: into a coffee bar in Boston or a block-long electronics store in Palo Alto, or into a taco shack in Austin, or a predictably twee organic food market in San Francisco. Think of it as you board airplanes beside guayabera-shirt-wearing 26-year-olds who sit in business class and could not explain to you what it is they do for a living if you gave them an hour and the use of a whiteboard. Think of it as you use your computer to check a stock at work or to send your granddaughter an electronic greeting card from a Web site your cousin in Ames, Iowa, told you about in an e-mail sent from an Alaskan cruise ship's business-affairs center. Think of it as you curse your bank and put your money into a higher risk 401(k) category instead, knowing, as we all do now, in the yettie era, that we're each and every one of us entitled—that it's our inalienable right to have!—a 20 percent return on investment.

Think of it when you go out to dinner, to some unambitious little restaurant on the newly gentrified side of town that caters to yetties as McDonald's does to their counterparts in the underclass. Watch those yetties close! It is neither the conspicuous consumption of the '80s nor the ironic inconspic-uous consumption of the early '90s—a scene comprised of smartest-guy-in-the-bar hipsters drinking Buds with their meaty rib dinners. Instead it's just people with money, dress-ing simply, living simply, working real hard, and considering themselves somehow a little above it all. It's a detached and unromantic upper-middle-class realism of the sort that a yettie's grandfather lived to the fullest in the flat sun of the Eisenhower '50's. Everyone's okay. Party's just droning on.

I talked to a friend about it recently.

"What a weird fate," he said.

And he's right. It's 10:15 in the evening and the food is of a sort with what you might have made at home if you weren't so interested in the chance and the ease to pay for the privi-lege. How's the food? Whatever: It's just $100; it's just fucking dinner. Ordered in, ordered out. Four, five nights a week.

Welcome to the new affluence. Welcome to our new yettie nation.

9

YETTIE SPEAK:
A GLOSSARY

LORD, HOW THEY TALK! What follows is by no means an encyclopedic glossary of yettie terms and phrases. It is instead a listing of some of the interesting words and phrases that, among the yetties, come up from time to time. Some of the terms are technical, but not many. Mostly this lingo is jargon and slang—a patois made up of business-speak and geek idiom and pop-cultural expression.

ACTION ITEM Something requiring immediate attention. The need for a lot more venture capital, for instance.

AMBIMOUSETEROUS Dude, that's cool: You can use your mouse with *either hand*!

APP Abbreviation of "application," or a computer program that performs a task, as Microsoft Word does word processing and Excel does spreadsheets. See "Killer app."

ASK A simply stated question, as when a programmer cuts a manager off with a brutal, "Look, what's your ask?"

BANDWIDTH Basically, bandwidth is time in the context of your modem and your Internet service provider's information-carrying capacity and speed. Mostly speed. Broad bandwidth: Your Internet connection at work. Narrow bandwidth: Your Internet connection at home, where the pictures of the sexy ladies take nine times as long to load. The term can also be applied to humans, viz., "I'd love to help you with that inordinately time-consuming project, fella, but I simply don't have the bandwidth." See also "Broadband."

BANDWIDTH JUNKIE The bandwidth junkie obsesses over increasing the speed of his Internet access. This is by no means exclusively a yettie trait. Bandwidth junkies spend a lot of time at home waiting for the DSL guy. That's no way to make money.

BELLS AND WHISTLES Web site features designed to impress the visitor (a potential investor, say) but that do little to improve the actual quality of the site. In fact, bells and whistles are often used to distract the viewer away from poor content.

BETA TEST The free release of a product not quite ready for public sale but good enough for a wider testing arena than the office pool of professional beta testers. A beta test should reveal bugs in programs that are almost finished, so that they may be fixed before the product ships to stores. Extremely coincidentally, beta testing is also a good marketing tool.

BIG PHARMA The really big drug companies, such as Procter & Gamble. A yettie might say, "We're courting Big Pharma on this interactive biotech thing."

BLUE CHIP An established company—and its stock—known for measured growth and market reliability. Rarely held in a yettie's portfolio.

BOOKMARK A Web browser can "bookmark" a Web site so that the user can return to it without retyping the site's URL. In the parlance, however, the word means "to take note of"— as in, "I bookmarked that guy when I met him at Comdex, and then hired him three months later."

BOOLEAN LOGIC A form of algebra in which all values are reduced to either "true" or "false." Named after the 19th-century mathematician George Boole, Boolean logic is especially important for computer science, because it combines well with the binary numbering system, in which each bit has a value of either 1 or 0. It's also used in search engines and is a good term for Nerds Made Good to drop into discussions with Neo-Yuppie Prepsters, who tend to respond to it with looks of stark fear.

BRAIN BAG An often ugly and always utilitarian hybrid of messenger bag and briefcase used to transport laptop computers and related ephemera, including spare batteries, modem cables, and disks.

BRAIN DUMP The process of explaining to the fellow replacing you at work exactly what it is you do every day in this job that you've just quit to go on to a much better one at another company across town, for more money and a better chance to make loads more money than that. Additionally, any explanation that takes more than 10 minutes.

BRANDING Marketing strategy used to make a company, or a company's name, instantly recognizable in a highly competitive, oversaturated marketplace.

BRANDWIDTH See "Branding." Then ask how successful the strategy was. Microsoft? Those kids have some *serious* brandwidth.

BRICK-AND-MORTAR An adjectival phrase used to evoke the 19th-century values of the Old Economy, when companies were built of warehouses and factories instead of bits and hype.

BROADBAND Technology that offers the transfer of multiple signals via a single conduit, allowing for high-speed information exchange. Serious bandwidth is the result of broadband technology. Colloquially, "the future," with your Internet, cable TV, and phone service all coming into the house through a big, fat pipe.

BROWSER A program that reads HTML pages via TCP/IP. "In other words, *Mom*, it's the screen that comes up on the computer I bought you, when you first access the World Wide

Web. The thing that shows you the top news of the day and lets you search the Internet for pictures of baby pandas? That's the browser."

BUG A small error in design or code in hardware or software. Also, the explanation for any secondary personality defect in a coworker.

BURGER A start-up company created in the hope that it can be sold—or "flipped"—before its underlying problems are discovered. Sayeth the yettie: "This is a burger company, man. No revenue, but high visibility in the submarket. Oracle's interested."

BURN RATE A calculation of the rate at which a company is spending its capital while waiting to become profitable. When a company's burn rate exceeds what it said it would be in the business plan, or when revenues fail to meet ex-pectations, the company scrambles for more capital. When this fails, it lays people off. When this fails, it goes out of business. Thinking about burn rate is a preoccupation of the yettie CEO.

BUZZWORD SPECIALIST That guy down the hall talking about "reintermediating out-of-the-box technologies," who very clearly has no idea what he's talking about, is a buzzword specialist. That he's also in marketing is a good bet.

CAMPUS In the Old Economy workers went to jobs in a plant or a store or a suite of offices. When they wanted a coffee, or a pack of cigarettes, or simply to take a walk, they left work and went out the door and into the world. In the New Economy, and particularly in Silicon Valley, companies are built on leafy parks that resemble college campuses. On campus, the work-er exists in a virtual world of in-house coffee bars and in-house health clubs and parklike areas with benches for cat-naps and sometimes even day beds in quiet rooms for real sleep. The employee need never leave the campus, and is therefore thought to be more productive.

CHAT The exchange of text between two or more connected computers in real time. Typed conversations, in other words, in which thought is generally secondary to response time.

CHAT ROOM The virtual space in which chats occur, usually involving a theme to tie together the participants. An interest in same-sex pornography, for instance. Or cats.

CHATTER'S BLOCK A condition marked by hyperanxiety about sending chat or instant messages, in which the user becomes so concerned with grammatical, syntactical, and topical perfection that he ends up typing nothing at all. Chatter's block is extremely rare, as a visit to any chat room will illustrate.

CLIENT/SERVER A computer that can run its own software and access a server only when it needs additional data. Also, a synonym for sex: "I had some client/server action with that cute product manager last night. Should I e-mail her today, or wait three?"

COBWEB SITE Refers to a Web site so devoid of fresh content that it has grown virtual cobwebs.

CODE Roughly, the instructions that make a particular program run. Code is the building block of the Internet and, one could argue, of the New Economy itself.

CODE 18 Any error made by the computer user, who is generally 18 inches from the monitor screen.

CODE MONKEY A programmer capable only of grinding out primitive work and incapable of performing more sophisticated operations. A studly programmer might say of a code monkey, and mean it, "He's an idiot."

CONTENT All those words on the Web page you visit during a down moment of work, the ones advertising all-in-one washer-dryer units or lingerie or bath products, all those paragraphs on other sites railing against the quality of this or that new technology, CD, movie, or political stance, all those pithy little tag lines for pornographic sites, and all those "help" windows that come up on your screen—all this is "content."

COOKIE A marker sent surreptitiously from a Web site to a browser that customizes future exchanges between the user and the site. Also, a Crossover Geezer's young girlfriend.

COOL Cross-platform yettie synonym for good, decent, awesome, groovy, all right, okay, nice, neat, sweet, keen, adequate, fair, acceptable. Unfortunate alternate spelling, meant to mimic the diction of an adolescent mall girl: kewl.

CRACKER An ill-intentioned hacker. Crackers break into— "crack"—computer systems in order to access, steal, or destroy sensitive information. "Cracker" is not a synonym for "hacker." Outside the yettie environment, however, the two words are often used as such, to the *incredible* dismay of the latter group. See "Hacker."

CRASH Any sudden, drastic failure—especially of a computer, or the stock market.

CUBE Alternate form of the word "cubicle," in which Mouse Jockeys toil over their monitors. See also "Geekosphere."

CUBE FARM A large, open office space filled with cubicle-bound yettie employees.

CYBERPUNK Originally a subgenre of science fiction, the term is now most often used to describe a small subspecies of the Mouse Jockeys: those leather-clad technocrats who speak in manifestos about the future of technology without really doing much to get there.

CYBERSPACE Mainstream jargon, meaning "the Internet."

CYBERSQUATTING The act of registering the domain name of a large, well-known, brick-and-mortar company before the company wises up and does so itself, in the hopes that the company will pay a large sum to buy back its own name for its own, way late, Web site. Increasingly rare, as large, well-known, brick-and-mortar companies have increasingly wised up to the need for Web sites.

DATABASE An ordered set of information. In the information-based New Economy, the immense database is king because it represents—albeit in ways the New Economy is still struggling to dope out—future profits.

DEAD No longer functioning. May refer to machines or, less often, to human beings.

DEAD TREE EDITION The hard, printed-on-paper copy of any given document.

DEADFISH, IDAHO A fictitious town invoked to conjure up an image of the single worst possible market for any given mass-produced soft- or hardware product. In Deadfish the residents are conformist knuckleheads with a singular lack of imagination and a deep aversion to both change and independent thought.

DEATH MARCH The final countdown to a product's shipping date, usually marked by the yettie involved in its creation in increments of 18-hour days.

DIGERATI A slickster media term for the digital elite.

DOC Diminutive of "document." A yettie's frequently updated résumé, for instance.

DOMAIN NAME A domain name locates a company, individual, or organization on the Internet. For example, www.rugmerchant.com locates the commercial e-rug seller Rugmerchant on the World Wide Web. In contrast, www.savetheemu.org locates the home page of the not-for-profit pro-emu organization Save the Emu.

DOMAINIST A person who judges others simply on the basis of their e-mail domains: "So the bunny gives me her home e-mail and it's, like, bunny@well.com, and I'm thinking, she's still in the *Well?*"

DOORSTOP A piece of broken or outmoded hardware kept around in the slight chance that it might be used in the future. Your Codewriting Geek, for instance, might have in his possession both a Commodore 64 and an Apple IIe.

DOT COMMUNIST A term that never really caught on in the yettie world, mostly because of the generally bankrupt nature of the word "communist." Libertarianism, or at any rate pseudolibertarianism, is the yettie's chief political interest. Self-described dot communists are uncommon.

DOWN Not functioning. Just at the moment when mainstream culture got used to the notion of "down" as a modern, rappy analogue of the jazzy "with it," the yetties went and changed everything.

DOUBLEGEEKING The act of using two computers at once.

DOWNLOAD To transfer data from a "host" to a "client," i.e., from a server to a PC. More colloquially, a CEO may download on his subordinates.

E- A prefix used to indicate virtually anything with an Internet root, from e-mail to e-commerce to the e-elite.

E-ELITE See "Digerati."

EGOSURF The act of using search engines on the Web to find sites or documents that mention one's own name.

E-MALINGER To cruise around the Web mindlessly looking at sites and sending e-mails, instead of doing one's job. Common among yetties experiencing a lame-duck period before starting a new job. Also among Mouse Jockeys.

EMOTICON A series of typed characters that, when viewed sideways, are meant to indicate the emotional state of the writer. Thus :) is a smiley face, and :(is a frowny face, and :-(is a frowny face with a nose and :-| is a straight face with a nose. It used to be that words themselves performed this task, except in the case of seventh-grade girls, who have always used hearts to dot their i's.

EQUITY The amount of the company that the employee "owns." In the New Economy, equity is most often not worth the paper it will never be printed on.

EYEBALLS Marketing slang for the number of people looking at a particular Web site at any given time, for whatever reason. A site wants more eyeballs, always.

FAT CLIENT A personal computer with a huge amount of memory and a large hard drive, used to store information that might otherwise take up space on a company's server. Pitch letters to possible investors, for instance.

FILTER Settings on a browser that prevent certain Web sites and certain types of Web sites—pornographic Web sites, for instance—from being accessed from an employee's computer. In the parlance, filters "suck."

FLAME To send someone an inflammatory e-mail message.

FLAME WAR A high-volume exchange of flames.

FORM FACTOR The physical size and shape of a device, originally used to describe the size of circuit boards, though increasingly deployed by Designer Girls as a synonym for the noun form of "design."

404 Not where you thought it was, so named for the "404 File Not Found" error message given by some Web browsers. Car keys often go 404.

FUTURE-PROOF A design or idea so revolutionary that technological advancements will not overtake it. It's rare that products described as future-proof actually are. One example, however: pre-sliced ham.

FUZZY LOGIC A type of logic that discerns more than simple true and false values. Used mostly for artificial intelligence applications and some spell-checking programs. Taken literally, fuzzy logic is also what a lesser Marketing Geek might use in attempting to explain a product to a new client.

GEEK Formerly a carnival performer known for stunts involving biting the heads off live chickens, snakes, and vermin. More currently, someone with a passion for computers and computer science, to the exclusion of other, more human interests. Context has determined the word's flavor for the past decade: In high school "geek" is a pejorative; in yettievilles of whatever size, it's a mark of high praise.

GEEKOCILE Broadly, the confusing, mysterious world inhabited by geeks. More narrowly, the home in which a programmer lives.

GEEKOSPHERE Broadly, the confusing, mysterious world inhabited by geeks. More narrowly, the cubicle in which a programmer works.

GET IT To understand the culture of the New Economy and its particulars. To be a yettie you have to "get it." The scare quotes are implied, except by Crossover Geezers, who still signal them with their fingers in conversation.

HACKER Any expert programmer possessed of deep intellectual curiosity and, often, greasy hair. May spend days at a computer terminal, divining the intricacies of a system or network or program, in order to make it better. See "Cracker."

HARDWIRED That which cannot be altered. Just as your Macintosh is hardwired to run the Apple operating system, for example, a yettie—particularly a yettie with more equity than you—may be hardwired to be an asshole.

HTML HyperText Markup Language. The standard computer language used to create pages on the Web. The Geek Literatus uses it to build Web sites, when he's not working on his novel at home.

HTTP HyperText Transfer Protocol. The way HTML files are recognized, read, and transferred by a computer and viewed by a browser. The bar over which the Geek Literatus must raise his work.

HIT A documented visit to a particular Web site. A site advertising free downloadable video footage of a graphic sexual act involving a celebrity might record a lot of hits; a how-to-clean-your-gutters site might not. Hits are an analogue of the Old Economy media term "readers."

INCUBATOR A company that helps develop, fund, and oftentimes house an Internet start-up company in the hope that the investment will pay off in spades.

INTERNET For the record, the Internet is the vast network of interconnected computers that use the TCP/IP protocol to exchange information. See also "World Wide Web," which is different.

INTERNET TIME The belief that everything on the Internet happens faster than anywhere else. Everything: the growth and decline of companies; the introduction of successive new technologies; the movement of information; the acquisition of wealth; even the length of time one "should" work for a company before leaving for another.

KILLER APP An application program that clinches the decision to purchase the system on which the application appears. The classic example is the spreadsheet program Lotus 1-2-3, which in many ways ("We-gotta-get-this-thing-it-comes-on-the-computer-you-gotta-buy-we-need-this-thing") introduced the personal computer to the business world. Developing a killer app can make a yettie very, very wealthy.

KLUDGE Any product or program thrown together without refinement, planning, or consideration of good design. In its adjectival form, *kludgey*.

KNOWLEDGE CAPITAL Self-help books for executives have led to yettie terms like this, which translates as intelligence and training combined.

KNOWLEDGE MANAGEMENT Another self-helpy term for executives, it is the act of keeping the smart people under control.

LISTSERV An automated e-mail address-list distribution system that often serves as a themed discussion group. Sure marker of a Nerd Made Good is membership in a listserv.

(THE) MATRIX Another synonym for Internet, this one taken from the 1999 Keanu Reeves vehicle of the same name.

MEATSPACE The "real world" of human interaction. Particularly for programmers and the brainier sort of Mouse Jockey, meatspace has nothing on the Matrix.

MEETING ENGINEER Anyone who appears to spend more time in meetings than he does actually working.

METRICS Originally understood as the statistical data included in user's manuals for software and hardware products, metrics is increasingly defined as any statistical data relating to the New Economy.

MODE Frame of mind. One could be in crunch mode, for instance, when finishing a product, or in stealth mode, when finishing a business plan, or in party mode, when breaking out the Fritos and microbrew.

MONITOR PET Any small stuffed animal or cartoon doll affixed to, or resting upon, a computer monitor.

MOORE'S LAW In 1965, Gordon Moore, cofounder of Intel, noted that the number of transistors per square inch on integrated circuits had doubled every year since the integrated circuit was invented. Moore's Law dictated that progress would continue at that rate. The pace has slowed, but not much: The current definition of Moore's Law, upheld by Moore himself, holds that data density will double every 18 months. From this sort of metrics comes the idea of Internet time.

MULTITASKING To perform several tasks at once, occasionally in the name of productivity. That slack tone in the voice of the yettie friend you called on the phone? He's checking his e-mail during the call. That clicking sound? He's answering his e-mail during the call.

NETIQUETTE Network etiquette, or the informal code of conduct that has evolved in cyberspace. Mostly at the hands of those who use emoticons in their e-mails. "Let's not start a flame war, people! :)"

NETIZEN A "citizen" of the Internet, or someone who uses networked resources. And emoticons in his e-mail.

NEWBIE A yettie neophyte, either to a company or to the use of a particular technology. Either way: "That guy's a newbie, so he doesn't know shit."

NEW PARADIGM An innovation that claims to alter the use of the Internet as we understand it. Virtually every new software product or Web site claims to provide a new paradigm.

NEWSGROUP An online discussion group based on a specific topic, such as Afrofuturism, or the band Ben Folds Five. Newsgroups, like the listservs they resemble, are a good place to find obsessive yetties.

NICKEL AND DIME, THE The 510 telephone area code for the east San Francisco Bay area, including Oakland and Berkeley. A yettie bedroom community.

NERD BIRD Any weekday direct flight to San Jose, California, particularly one from Austin, Texas.

NONLINEAR Verb meaning to erupt in uncontrollable—and often illogical—anger.

OFFLINE In private: "Let's talk about this offline."

OUTSOURCE A New Economy cost-cutting technique, in which freelancers, or other companies, perform tasks that the company outsourcing the work doesn't want contributing to its overhead. Outsource your payroll, your human resources department, even your programming! Lean and mean is the New Economy way.

PERMATEMP On the West Coast a permatemp is someone who has put in years of temp work at the same company without ever getting hired full-time or receiving health benefits. On the East Coast permatemping means putting in years of temp work at many, many different companies without ever getting hired full-time or receiving health benefits.

PHREAKING The act of cracking a phone system, usually to make long-distance calls for free.

PRAIRIE-DOGGING A series of heads popping up from cubicles throughout a cube farm, usually in reaction to a dramatic stimulus along the lines of a loud argument, or a Salesbot hurling a chair in frustration.

RAMP UP To prepare, gear up, get ready—quickly.

RANDOM Any poorly reasoned argument.

SCALABILITY The ability to grow quickly to match a company's increased needs, as when a Web site's traffic increases from 300 hits a week to 300 a minute without crashing. That's scalability.

SCROLL LOCK The key that turns the scroll lock light on and off on a computer keyboard.

SERVER A computer that supplies data and applications for the use of other computers.

SHAREWARE A sluttish yettie may be described as such.

SILICON VALLEY FOOD STAMP A $50 bill.

STICKINESS That ineffable something that gives a Web site returning eyeballs and lots of hits.

SUDDEN-WEALTH SYNDROME Getting too rich too quick. The yettie who buys a 5,600-square-foot house, then sleeps on a futon in the living room for a year, with a Testa Rossa moldering in the garage because he can't drive stick, is a good example.

THREAD Generally used to denote a line of discussion on a listserv or in a chat room.

TRAFFIC The load on a communications device or a system. Heavy traffic is a good thing on a Web site, but for the user heavy traffic can mean slowdowns in load times, as thousands attempt to retrieve the same information at the same time over the same wires.

UNINSTALLED To be fired or laid off.

UNSTRUNG No wires! A catchall term for wireless Internet applications and technology.

UPGRADE To replace a current version of a software program with a newer or enhanced version; or, in the case of hardware, adding more memory; or, in the case of a boyfriend, to move from a programmer to a CIO.

VAPORWARE Software that doesn't exist, despite all the marketing that has gone into selling it.

VESTING Pejorative term in large companies, used to refer to an employee's slacking off in the months just prior to the actual vesting of his stock options, at which point he will undoubtedly sell and retire. Thus: "I wouldn't expect too much help from Zack; he's vesting."

WHITEBOARD A white plastic blackboard, used for brain-storming. It is the collective mind of a start-up, its crutch and memory and tool all combined. Also, an application allowing several networked users to update the same document in real time.

WORLD WIDE WEB A section of the Internet that presents information through linked graphical pages maintained by both public and privately owned computers around the world. You ought to know that by now.

YESTERDAY In the New Economy, "now."

10

ACRONYMS:
LIFE IN THE A.R.E.

THAT YETTIES LIVE IN an acronym-rich environment is a function of both their geeky past and a present filled with e-mail and instant-messaging chat. Computer science is filled with acronyms. The grandfather of the Internet was a government-funded research project called the Advanced Research Project Agency Network, more conveniently known as ARPANET. Some yetties grew up writing programs in Beginner's All-Purpose Symbolic Instruction Code, more conveniently known as BASIC. Some grew up to program in Hypertext Markup Language, or HTML, and followed the dictates of the HyperText Transfer Protocol, or HTTP, so that the files could be recognized and read on the Web. When your aunt sends you, via e-mail, a compressed photo file of your nephew getting his first haircut, it comes marked as a JPEG file, for the Joint Photographic Experts Group that developed the method of compression. There are literally thousands of examples. If a yettie didn't use acronyms there wouldn't be much time in his day to browse new mountain bikes online.

For similar reasons, yetties use a lot of acronyms in their e-mail-based communications. These have the same simple, childlike flavor of emoticons, and are used for the same reason: to convey, in code, what words used to. In some cases the acronyms have moved over into the spoken language, as a sort of shortcut to understanding. In these cases the acronyms are generally given a sarcastic edge. Thus LOL, which in an e-mail means "laughing out loud," becomes, in an office setting—standing around the latte machine, for instance—L...O...L, or "That's not funny at all."

This list is nowhere near comprehensive. New acronyms are created every day, while others are retired. It is simply a catch basin of a few of the acronyms you're likely to come across while stalking the dot-com geek.

AFAIK As Far As I Know. Used in e-mail as a hedge against accountability.

AFK Away From Keyboard. Used to explain an otherwise unexplained absence during an instant-messaging "conversation."

AI Artificial Intelligence. When the robots finally come and ask for our children and our wealth, it will be because we programmed them to think, and to learn, with artificial intelligence.

AIIC As If I Care. Used in e-mail to convey insouciance.

AISI As I See It. Used in e-mail to indicate either the beginning or end of a stated opinion.

ANFAWFOS And Now For A Word From Our Sponsor. Used in e-mail to show pop-cultural awareness and a childlike clarity about how the world operates. Usually followed by a break from the keyboard.

ASAFP As Soon As Fucking Possible. Not so much a command as an answer, viz., "When are you going to leave that job?"

ASL Age? Sex? Location? A standard chat query despite the low probability of veracity in the standard answer: "22, F, in bed."

ASP Application Service Provider. A company that stores its hardware and software in a remote location and leases the programs' use to customers over the Internet. ASP is a kind of B2B, for which, see below.

B2B Business to Business. A company that provides a product or service to another company.

B2C Business to Consumer. A company that provides a product or service to individuals. What was called in the Old Economy a "store."

BAD Broken As Designed. A computer program that, either by accident or design, does not perform particular tasks or lacks certain features.

BAIC Boy, Am I Confused. An acronym used in e-mail to indicate imminent repetition of an argument.

BBIAB Be Back In A Bit. Instant-messaging send-off, as the sender takes a phone call, or heads off to the bathroom, or shows his boss the project he was meant to have finished yesterday.

BBS Bulletin Board System. An online meeting and discussion area that allows people to carry on discussions and trade files without being connected to the network at the same time.

BRS Big Red Switch. A panic button. What the e-mailer hit when he heard that the company's incandescent burn rate would lead to employees getting uninstalled all over the place.

BSP Business Service Provider. A B2BASP.

BTW By The Way. Used in e-mail as the "P.S." was in old-style pen-and-ink correspondence. Also used as a transition statement.

BMW Bavarian Motor Works. Car, German, favored by senior management.

CLM Career Limiting Move. A rash action that places one's prospects of corporate advancement in jeopardy.

DP Data Processing.

DPI Dots Per Inch. A term used to describe image resolution in printers and flat monitors. The goal is to have a high DPI so that the dots making up images blend to create the illusion of a solid block. Designer Girls love the high DPI.

DSL Digital Subscriber Line. A form of high-speed Internet access that works over standard phone lines.

E2EG Ear-to-Ear Grin. Used in e-mail and instant-messaging to respond to high praise.

EAK Eating at keyboard. Falls under the category of TMI.

EOL End of lecture. Used at the conclusion of a particularly lengthy e-mail or chat rejoinder.

F/X Special effects. The bells and whistles used to bedazzle a Web site's visitors.

FAQ Frequently Asked Questions. A Web document that lists and answers common questions on a particular subject, usually created by people who are tired of answering the same questions over and over.

FIFO First In, First Out. More obliquely, the linear protocol system that governs information processing, such as which document in a queue a printer prints first.

FLA Four-Letter Acronym.

FTL Faster Than Light. Used to describe machines that are particularly fast.

FTP File Transfer Protocol. One of the first applications developed for ARPANET, FTP remains the protocol by which Internet files are sent and retrieved.

FUBAR Fucked Up Beyond Recognition. Used in reference to software and hardware and, to a lesser extent, to coworkers after the office party.

FWIW For What It's Worth. E-mail hedge against embarrassment if the correspondent scorns your advice.

FYI For Your Information. Formerly an acronym that appeared only on sticky tags attached to newspaper and magazine articles, it now appears in the subject heading of e-mails containing attached files from newspaper or magazine Web sites.

FYIV Fuck You, I'm Vested. A Microsoft epithet, always used with a soupçon of Gatesian arrogance, meaning *I don't have to work.* Outside of Microsoft and a few of the other Big Name outfits, it falls under the category of False Bravado.

GIGO Garbage In, Garbage Out. A response to complaints that a program "doesn't work" when given poor input.

HTML Hypertext Markup Language. The programming language used to create pages on the World Wide Web.

HTTP HyperText Transfer Protocol. The way HTML files are recognized, read, and transferred by a computer and viewed by a browser.

IM Instant Messaging. A form of Web-based communication that allows people to waste inordinate amounts of time in the workplace and at home by chatting over the Internet in real time.

IMHO In My Humble Opinion. Used in both e-mail and actual conversation in exactly the same manner as when a clerk at an independent video store offers his opinion of a film.

IP Internet Protocol. The way computers identify themselves over the Internet.

IPO Initial Public Offering. Or Imminent Public Obscenity.

IRL In Real Life. What happens in meatspace.

IT Information Technology. Computers, basically.

IYFEG Insert Your Favorite Ethnic Group. Used while telling a bad joke in an e-mail, so as not to offend anyone in particular —and, in doing so, ruining the joke.

IUD Insert Usual Disclaimers. Hedge against the success of advice given in a particular e-mail.

KISS Keep It Simple, Stupid. Advice rarely taken.

L8R Later. Used as an e-mail sign-off.

LAN Local Area Network. A group of computers at a single location connected by phone lines or coaxial cable.

LOL Laughing Out Loud. Generally accompanied by an emoticon, LOL indicates the receipt of humor in an e-mail.

LRF Little rubber feet. The part of your printer that keeps it from slipping off the desk.

MUD Multi-User Dungeon. A real-time chat area in which participants conduct virtual-reality role-playing games.

MUSE Multi-User Simulated Environment. A MUD without the violence.

NDA Non-Disclosure Agreement. A contract preventing employees, freelancers, journalists, lawyers, the cleaning crew, and basically anyone who comes onto the campus from sharing or capitalizing on any of a company's intellectual property.

NFC No Fucking Clue. Quick negative answer to an e-mailed question.

NPVA No Practical Vertical Application. Applied to a person good only for sex.

PDA Personal digital assistant. Also known as a handheld or palmtop computer.

PFM Pure Freaking Magic. In other words, how something works.

P2P Path to Profitability. This is what the VC wants to see from your company, before you get a dime of his money. Alternatively, Peer to Peer, as when two Internet users perform a transaction without benefit of a middleman. Trade music files, for instance.

RFR Really Fucking Rich.

RFS Really Fucking Soon. Might be used in conjunction with RFR.

ROFL Rolling On the Floor Laughing. See LOL, then multiply.

RTFM Read The Fucking Manual. E-mailed response to an obtuse question about the operation of a particular machine or application. Not often sent, but often thought.

SAR Some Assembly Required. An understatement, used in e-mail to describe the difficulty of a particular new task.

TLA Three-Letter Acronym.

TMI Too Much Information. Used to indicate displeasure, as when an e-mail correspondent offers a long anecdote about personal hygiene or family dysfunction.

TPSM Traditional Page-Sequencing Method. That is to say, numbering pages from left to right and turning them from right to left while reading. Not all dead-tree publications subscribe to this method, particularly on the fringes of yettie culture.

URL Uniform Resource Locator. The address used by browsers to find resources on the Web.

VR Virtual Reality. A reality that does not in fact exist, but that looks and feels very real indeed.

WAP Wireless Application Protocol. A proposed standard for the secure transfer of information between wireless devices such as PDAs, cell phones, and pagers.

WOMBAT Waste Of Money, Brains, And Time. A project with no practical application or marketability.

YMMV Your Mileage May Vary. Caveat offered to any recommendation made.

Y2K Year 2000. Extremely clever marketing scheme.

The author and publisher would like to thank the following
people for their participation:

Dan Ackerman   Jenny Kubo
Waris Ahlhwalia   Owen Levin
Michael Brandt   Alison Lowenstein
Zeke Brill   Jennifer Moore
Pat Charles   Robert Nuell
Farley Chase   Jay Peterson
Danielle Davis   Cathy Riva
Kelly Del Ponti   Sarah Shatz
Kathleen Faherty   Yis Tigay
Chris Kavanaugh   Greg Tribbe
David Komurek   Mike Wolf
Elliott Kaufman

The publisher would also like to thank: Ericsson, Nokia, IBM, Sony Music,
Motorola, Brooks Brothers, Banana Republic, Nike, Time Will Tell,
Oliver Peoples, Paul Smith, What Comes Around Goes Around,
Alice Underground, Buffalo Chips, Jack Spade, and Samsung.